A *Seat* in the *Heavenlies*

LORD, Show Us How to Pray

SECOND EDITION

C.A. Archer

COURIER
PUBLISHING

A Seat in the Heavenlies: LORD, Show Us How to Pray

Second Edition © 2024 C.A. Archer

ISBN: 978-1-955295-43-7 (softcover)
ISBN: 978-1-955295-44-4 (hardcover)
ISBN: 978-1-955295-45-1 (e-book)

Library of Congress Control Number: 2021907493

Courier Publishing
100 Manly Street
Greenville, South Carolina 29601
CourierPublishing.com

PUBLISHED IN THE UNITED STATES OF AMERICA

Thank you to the people who made
this book a reality:

My granddaughter, Aubrey — who partnered with me
to verify hundreds of biblical references

Michael — for your encouragement to write, your time
investment, and doctrinal input

Bonnie, Missy, and Angela — for your most excellent proofreading

My daughters, Tera, Jennifer, and Kara —
for your encouragement and honest advice

My husband, Elliott — for his insight,
reassurances during discouragement
and his very astute observations

Introduction

For many years of my Christian life, I did not understand prayer. It was a mystery to me. I loved the Bible, but my experience of prayer was a thousand miles from the prayer I saw described in it. I knew I should pray, would try to pray, and desperately wanted to pray; but it was like making a phone call where I was never quite sure if there was anyone on the other end of the line or not. If I prayed out loud, as a friend suggested, I would feel silly. But if I prayed silently, my mind would wander, and I would end up thinking about things like whether or not Pittsburgh would make it to the Super Bowl.

I had dozens of questions over the years. Why did I feel so reluctant to pray? Why was prayer the easiest discipline to ignore and the hardest to practice? Why did I either pray for the same things over and over again, or else run out of things to say? Why did I have so little expectation that God would hear and answer? Why did I feel so far away from Him — like my prayer didn't even rise above the ceiling, let alone ascend to Heaven?

I remember reading Matthew 21:21-22, the passage that says if we ask with enough faith, we can cast a mountain into the sea and have anything we ask for in prayer. What!? Prayer so effective you could order a mountain into the sea!? I was a person who got bored and discouraged from a 30-minute prayer meeting — and we're talking about moving mountains? If this Scripture was the measure of the prayer expected from me, I would be defeated before I even started.

It seemed to me that the Scriptures made a lot of claims about prayer that were not only beyond my experience, but hard to believe. Yet the more confused I was about the matter, the more I yearned to talk to God as Abraham did — friend to friend.

Then one day, totally by chance, I was reading and came across a quote that changed my whole way of thinking. Richard Foster, theologian and author of *Celebration of Discipline,* wrote:

> I determined to learn to pray so that my experience conformed to the words of Jesus rather than try to make His words conform to my impoverished experience.

A light came on in my soul. Foster had absolutely, oh-so-accurately, described my frustrating prayer life. I had an up-side down, unsatisfying, ineffective, impoverished experience of prayer because I had never concerned myself with *conforming my prayer to the words of Jesus and to the words of the Scriptures He authenticated.*

I had read the Bible somewhat regularly for years, but after pondering this quote, I began to read it looking for anything connected with prayer. Each time I found something, I would mark it with a yellow highlighter and simply turn to God in my heart with the attitude, "LORD, I want to learn to pray like this. Would you show me how to pray?"

Father,

You told Jeremiah, "Call to me and I will answer you and tell you great and unsearchable things you do not know" [Jer. 33:3]. LORD, I want that same thing. I want you to tell ME great and unsearchable things! And anyone who takes the time to read this book wants them too. So many of us are shriveling on the vine for want of this.

Father, will you show us how to pray?

Day 1

*Who is he that condemns? Christ Jesus who died
— more than that, who was raised to life — is at the
right hand of God and is also interceding for us.*
— Romans 8:34

*And God raised us up with Christ and seated us with
him in the heavenly realms in Christ Jesus.*
— Ephesians 2:6a

Where are we when we pray? I don't mean physically. I mean spiritually. The verses in the above text say Christ is currently seated at God's right-hand and interceding for us. And we are seated with Him. If that fact is a little hard to understand, let's consider a political illustration. There are one hundred desks in the US Senate. When new senators come in, they receive specific desks and, by tradition, write their names on the inside or on the bottom. We could say they are *seated in the Senate*. If they are in office, no matter where they are physically (they could be in their home states, in recess, or on business somewhere in the world) they enjoy the privileges, honor, responsibility, and voice of that seat.

In the same way, there is only one seat at the right hand of Almighty God. It is occupied by Jesus Christ who advocates and intercedes for us. Since the resurrection, Christ has been granted all authority in heaven and on earth (Matt. 28:18) and He effectually conducts all Kingdom business with God the Father from this seat.

As we step into a ninety-day-long devotional on prayer, here is an amazing truth: According to Ephesians 2:6, believers have the insurmountable privilege to sit with Christ in His seat at the right hand of the God of the Universe and comingle our prayer with His! Every believer sits uniquely placed — by the sovereign plan of God — in a positional, spiritual reality where we are invited to be actively involved in the intercession that brings down the "immeasurable riches of his grace in kindness toward us in Christ Jesus" (Eph. 2:7).

Prayer takes on a whole new dimension when we can grasp these truths. It's amazing! Christ is at this very moment seated at the right hand of God the Father, and we are seated with Him and in Him. It monumentally makes a difference when we realize God is calling us to warm, intimate, real relationship and interaction with Himself. He is calling us to the greatest and highest privilege we can ever be involved in. He is calling us to the practice of Scripture-based prayer — prayer with some teeth in it. He is inviting us to sit with Jesus in the heavenlies and do what Jesus does without ceasing — interceding with the Father.

LORD,

It makes a huge difference when we understand where we are when we pray. We're not light years away from You! We are at Your right hand in Christ. He shares with us the privilege, honor, responsibility, and voice of His seat. Thank You for this incredible truth, and help us to be aware, every time we approach You, that we are praying from our position — in Christ — in heavenly realms. We are as close as Your own right hand. Amen.

Day 2

In the sermon on the mount, Jesus said,
"This is how you should pray."
— Matthew 6:9a

So, what is our starting point in God showing us how to pray? What are the first critical concepts He wants us to know? A logical place to begin would be with the instruction we find in Matthew 6:9-13, which is commonly referred to as the Lord's Prayer. Many of us can quote the substance of it from the days of our childhood, as we repeated the King James Version:

> Our Father, who art in heaven,
> Hallowed be thy name.
> Thy kingdom come, Thy will be done on earth as it is in heaven.
> Give us this day our daily bread.
> Forgive us our debts, as we forgive our debtors.
> And lead us not into temptation, but deliver us from evil.
> For thine is the kingdom, and the power, and the glory, forever. Amen.

Of course, designating these verses as the Lord's Prayer is a little misleading, because this is really the disciples' prayer: a model, a pattern, and a blueprint for the believers to follow when they pray. This model prayer is not a mantra to be mechanically and ritualistically repeated over and over until it loses its meaning. It is rather a *succinct list of topics for believers to address when we pray.* Just as Ephesians 2:6 tells us where we are when we pray, the model prayer tells us *what to pray for.*

Despite its brevity, there is tremendous depth, width, and possibility in the model prayer. We are to address each topic and flesh it out with the details of our own life experiences and needs as we walk with the Lord. Paul, for example, in Romans 11:33-36, prays a magnificent doxology that ends, "For from him and through him and to him are all things. To him be the glory forever! Amen" (Rom. 11:36).

Here's what Paul is actually doing: He's taking the topic of hallowing God's name, according to the pattern of the model prayer, and pouring it out in real, living, passionate adoration of the God he is doing life with. He is not offering up to God a stale, distanced, rote repetition of Jesus's instructions. He is offering up the response of a heart that genuinely hallows the name of God.

Here's a bold statement: The prayers that the Holy Spirit records in Scripture all correspond in one way or another to one or more of the elements (topics) in the model prayer. Let's begin this book by looking at them.

Father,

    Jesus takes a subject that has more depth and possibility than any other discipline known to man and breaks it down into a pattern that is understandable, doable, and applicable to all of life. Prayer that is organized according to these topics fits the needs of believers like hands fit gloves.

As we look at each of these elements of the model prayer in the following entries, may we learn to build deep and wide on them, because it is the model You use to show us how to pray. Help us to see the ENORMITY this pattern of prayer allows.

"The Lord's prayer takes less than twenty seconds to read aloud, but it takes a lifetime to learn."

— Al Mohler

Day 3

This, then, is how you should pray:
"Our Father in heaven ..."
— Matthew 6:9

There's a famous photo taken in 1963 by *Look* magazine photographer, Stanley Tretick, of John F. Kennedy Jr. hiding under his father's desk in the Oval Office. President Kennedy was the most powerful man in the world at the time. No other children on earth had the privilege of playing under his desk — only his own son and daughter. Their relationship to JFK gave them access to him. We have access to our Father in prayer because of our relationship with Him through our faith in Jesus Christ.

One of the first ministries of the Holy Spirit we become aware of when we become believers is the sense of being God's children. He allows us to *"cry Abba Father"* (Rom. 8:15). So, it's not surprising the first topic in the model prayer is how believers are to address the Almighty Omnipotent God; we are to address Him as "Father."

What a sense of security! Our Father! He is the sovereign Master of All Things. He is all-powerful. There's nothing He can't do. There's not a single thing in this universe — not war, not disease, not disaster, not loneliness, not poverty, not aging, and not death itself — that we need to fear because our Father is always in control.

It's interesting that in this first topic of prayer, Jesus addresses the

8

issue of who we are. No more trying to find ourselves, trying to prove ourselves, or looking for affirmation from the world around us to give us a sense of worth. We finally know our true identity. Our significance comes from our relationship with our Father. We are children of God, and He works in us through all the issues of life to conform us to Jesus Christ so that we can be who we are — we can actually live it out. Every time we open prayer with the words, "Our Father" we are reminded of these truths.

> How great is the love the Father has lavished on us, that we
> should be called children of God! And that
> is what we are! The reason the world
> does not know us is that it did not know him. (1 John 3:1)

There is no more secure position in the entire universe than to be a child of God. We express our dependence on Him, our love for Him, our need for Him and our security in Him every time we pray and open the dialogue by addressing Him as Father.

Let's pray that we would grasp the unspeakable
wonder of praying to a perfect and loving Father.

Father,

Thank You for this first lesson in showing us how to pray. We are to call on You as our Father. All our lives we've struggled with feelings of insecurity and the yearning for significance. But just whispering Father when we address You in prayer reminds us of who we really are — that we are the children of Deity. We belong to You. The question of our most basic identity is addressed in how we are to approach You in prayer. We love being Your child.

Dear friends, now we are children of God, and what we will be has not yet been made known. But we know that when Christ appears, we shall be like him, for we shall see him as he is (1 John 3:2).

Day 4

Hallowed be your name.
— *Matthew 6:9*

Does the LORD need our worship in order to feel good about Himself, as some atheistic thinkers have suggested? Is His self-image dependent on what we think?

Not at all. God the Father does not need our worship, our praise, or our thanks. He is totally self-existent and does not need the opinion of created beings to affirm Him. Jesus does not instruct us to hallow the Father's name because the Father needs it — Jesus instructs us to hallow the Father's name because we need it! We need a worthy center around which our souls revolve for all eternity. Without this God-centric element in our lives, we become like one of the old agitator washers that get out of balance and, if not repaired, eventually just chew themselves up and quit working. People simply cannot live without God at the center — without Him, everything eventually falls apart.

To hallow God the Father is to reverence Him as holy. It is to recognize there is no one like Almighty God. He is both infinite and ultimate. We could call this the **communing aspect** of prayer, where we communicate to Him our worship, our praise, our thanks, and our reverence. We are letting Him know we recognize who He is, and that our view and understanding of Him is formed by what He says about

11

Himself in Scripture. We are expressing that we believe what He tells us about Himself.

As we commune with Him, wonderful things happen to us. God is placed in the center of our lives where He should be. Communing prayer prepares us for the other aspects of prayer where we make requests of the Lord. It lifts us out of the pit of depression and discouragement because it's impossible to worship God and be discouraged and depressed at the same time.

Communing prayer restores a Biblical perspective in our current circumstances. As we praise and worship, it draws us up to the throne of grace so that we see things as God sees them; we see them in light of God's power instead of our own weakness. This eternal perspective produces a very calming mindset, which settles the soul. Joy, peace, and delight bubble up as we are reminded of who and what God is; enthusiasm and passion for life and ministry are renewed because we realize — Wow! This is just the God we need! This is just the one to center our lives around. This is the one worthy of our complete allegiance and emulation. We realize that what we really yearn for — down deep in our souls — is God Himself.

Communing prayer is fed by Scripture as we read God's revelation of Himself. Our response of worship or praise or thanksgiving — expressed to Him — is extremely satisfying and strength-building. It is the really fun part of prayer, and although we may at first feel awkward and hesitant, as we continue in it, our enthusiasm builds and increases and overflows in sweet fellowship with the Father. Communing prayer may well be the activity which affords us the most satisfaction in the LORD. May we never cut it short.

Let's pray that we all truly hallow God's name, and that the day will come when His name is hallowed all over the earth.

Father,

You are our help! You are our strength! You are our Great Treasure! We love telling You these things — worshiping, praising, and thanking You for everything You do and everything You are. We love meditating on these things and grasping what they mean in our lives. Father, You are using communing prayer to teach us that no matter what our current circumstances — hallowing Your name leaves us with the sense that all is well. Everything is under control because You are the center of our being.

Day 5

This is how you should pray: Our Father in heaven, hallowed be your name, your kingdom come, your will be done on earth as it is in heaven.
— Matthew 6:9-10

It is a natural and easy thing to come into the LORD's presence and petition Him for the present physical needs and trials of ourselves and others. Praying for physical concerns is a wonderful privilege of prayer, and there are examples of such petitions in Scripture; but the physical affairs of this present world are not the kind of prayer referred to in the verse above.

Matthew 6:10 is addressing prayer that deals with God's eternal, as well as His present, agenda and goals. Let's call it **spiritual intercession.** So spiritual intercession has two applications in view: (1) His agenda for eternal things, and (2) His agenda for the present.

For God's **eternal agenda**, we are to pray for the day Christ comes again, takes up His throne in His Father's Kingdom, and we see the Father's will done on earth just like it is in heaven. When Isaiah cried out in Is. 64:1 for God to rip the heavens apart and come, he was praying according to the topic of Matt. 6:10 for God's eternal agenda. When David prays in Psalm 7:6-9, asking God to come and rule in utter justice, to put away wickedness and make His people utterly secure, he, too, is praying for this topic in the ultimate sense. Even in the next-to-the-last verse in the Bible, John the Apostle prays, "Amen. Come Lord Jesus" (Rev. 22:20). John is praying according to the topic of Matt. 6:10 with the ultimate agenda in mind.

In praying for God's **present agenda**, we are to pray specifically for every step along the way as God is in the process of bringing His Kingdom to earth. Spiritual intercession goes to the Word, finds what it needs for Kingdom business, and asks God to provide it — *for specific people, specific needs, and specific situations*. When Mary accepted what God had for her and prayed, "be it unto me according to thy word" (Luke 1:38 KJV); when Daniel pleaded God's promise for the exiles to return from Babylon and prayed, "For Your sake, O Lord, look with favor on Your desolate sanctuary" (Daniel 9:17); when Paul prayed for the Ephesian church, "That the God of our Lord Jesus Christ, the Father of glory, may give You the spirit of wisdom and revelation in the knowledge of him" (Eph. 1:17 KJV) — they were all praying spiritual intercession with the present view in mind. When we teach the Word of God in a small group setting and then pray for it to not return void, but to be effective, we are praying spiritual intercession. We are praying for specific steps that will ultimately bring in the coming Kingdom.

Spiritual intercession has some unique characteristics: (1) Even though it should (and often does) overlap with physical, present-world needs, it primarily has eternal, spiritual issues in mind. (2) It is fueled by Scripture — the promises, the precepts, and the purposes of God. We plead these things as we pray for specific needs we see spiritually.

The majority of prayer in the Bible is either communing prayer, which hallows God's name (praise, worship, and thanks) or spiritual intercession (asking God to do what He has willed or promised or purposed). Should it not occupy a lot of our prayer, too?

It should interest us that spiritual intercession is a very powerful aspect of prayer, because when we pray according to the promises and the revealed will of God in the Bible — motivated by desire to see His agenda and goals accomplished — ***His answer is always yes or wait.***

Father,

Your Word is a goldmine for the believer. We love the idea that we can go there to obtain all that we need regarding spiritual matters for ourselves and others. We advance the kingdom when we do this. In fact, every time we pray Scripture, we are, in a sense, making a withdrawal from the funds You've provided for Your purposes. Help us to understand this concept and comprehend the power You have made available to us.

"Oh God, thou hast given us a mighty weapon, and we have permitted it to rust. Thou hast given us that which is mighty as thyself, and we have let that power lie dormant."

— C.H. Spurgeon

1834–1892

Ah, Father God, may we not let it lie dormant! Or rust! May we realize that the weapon You have put in our hands accesses Your omnipotence!

Day 6

Give us today our daily bread.
— Matthew 6:11

I doubt if anyone reading this book is free from the troubles of life. We live in a physical world with needs, problems, sorrows, trials, illnesses and difficulties of every description. It's easy to understand why praying according to this fourth topic of prayer — referred to in Matt. 6:11 — probably occupies the most often repeated petitions in today's Church. Because asking God for the things that deal with the issues of our present physical life — our needs — we could refer to this type of prayer as **temporal petition.**

One of the wonders we can worship God for daily is that He doesn't pat us on the head after our salvation and leave us like orphans in a threatening world. He doesn't exhibit the attitude that we're on our own now, and we should handle things as best we can until He comes back for us later. No — "God is our refuge and strength, an ever-present help in trouble" (Ps. 46:1).

Unlike spiritual intercession, temporal petition is not confined to the eternal and spiritual realm. It is God's means of availing ourselves of His help in procuring our physical needs in the present. But there are a few Biblical truths we should keep in mind.

First, God has purpose for the different trials we go through. He uses painful situations to make us Christ-like (Rom. 8:29) and to purify our faith (1 Pet. 1:6, 7). To shorten or remove trial too soon would result in something not really for our good or His glory. He often wants us to trust Him IN the trial.

Second, God's answer to our temporal petitions can be *yes*, it can be *no*, or it can be *wait*. Hezekiah asked God for more years of life, and God said yes (2 Kings 20:1-7). Paul asked for a physical malady to be removed, but God said *no* (2 Cor. 12-1-7). When the church in Acts asked for Peter to be released from prison, God said *yes* (Acts 12:5-10). It was very probable that the church prayed similarly for the Apostle James, but God allowed James to be killed.

Third, God does not save us so that we have an easy, comfortable, problem-free life on this earth. This life is spiritual boot-camp. It is spiritual warfare, the training ground for transforming us into the likeness of Christ. We can come to the LORD, our Father, and ask Him for what we need — and often what we *think* we need, and He often graciously gives it — but temporal petition calls for the same attitude Jesus had when He asked for the cup of suffering in the crucifixion to pass from Him: "... nevertheless, not my will, but thine, be done" (Luke 22:42 KJV). It should not be a traumatic thing for believers when God says *no* or *wait* to our temporal petitions. He loves us and will not allow us to be tried beyond what we can handle but gives us a way to escape so that we can endure (1 Cor. 10:13). We can look to the following Scriptures for encouragement:

- He comforts us. (2 Cor. 1:3-4)
- He gives His angels charge over us. (Ps. 91:11)
- He never leaves us (although the trial sometimes is so great it feels like it!). (Heb. 13:5-6)
- He delivers us. (Ps. 34:19)
- He brings things together for our good. (Rom. 8:28)
- He listens to our prayer. (Ps. 116:2)
- He has pity on us as fathers pity their sons. (Ps. 103:13)
- There is nothing too hard for the LORD. (Jer. 32:27)

Let's pray that we would not lose heart when God seemingly says "no" to our temporal petitions and we would rest peacefully, trusting God while we wait on His answers.

Father,

Help us learn the disciplines of patience and perseverance, and supply our real needs as we wait on You. Thank You for hearing our weakest cries.

Day 7

Forgive us our debts, as we
also have forgiven our debtors.
— Matthew 6:12

Back in the Dark Ages of sending mail through the post office, we would sometimes receive letters with a post-script — a pertinent detail that had been left out of the body of the letter. Like, "Dear Clara, I will be arriving on the late train Sunday night. Love, Bob." Then, "P.S. The train doesn't get in until after 10:00 pm."

The topic of Matt. 6:12 is asking forgiveness for our own sins and forgiving others. It could be called the **confessionary aspect** of prayer, and it is the only petition in the model prayer with a post-script. Matt. 6:14-15 says:

> For if you forgive others their trespasses, your heavenly Father will also forgive you, but if you do not forgive others their trespasses, neither will your Father forgive your trespasses.

In my own case, Matt. 6:12 was a very neglected aspect of my prayer life, and doubtless one of the major reasons I felt so far from God when I tried to pray. It's amazing how much we can rationalize and ignore our own sin!

Matt. 6:12 is referring to asking forgiveness for the sins we commit as believers. If we do not confess, repent, and ask forgiveness, the relationship with God in prayer is hindered. The "postscript" indicates that refusing to forgive others is connected with God forgiving us. Prayer is hindered when we refuse to deal with either one of these issues.

Confessing sin is a wonderfully freeing exercise. It demands a tender heart and an honest response to the conviction of the Holy Spirit as He deals with us when we pray. But the great news is, if we ask forgiveness for our own sin and forgive those who sin against us, we are freed from the pretense of presenting ourselves to God as if everything is fine between us, when both we and God know it is not. We don't have to hide from our Father.

So, we must make a choice: Do we want to hang on to our unforgiveness and the sin the Holy Spirit convicts us of when we come to God in prayer, or do we want the delight of an intimate, warm, prayer-answering relationship with God? We can't have both.

Pray for the world-wide Church, our own congregations, our pastor(s), our leaders, our teachers, and ourselves that:

- We not neglect this aspect of prayer; that we keep short accounts; that we not be afraid to confess things to God, even though sometimes it seems we struggle with certain sins and find ourselves confessing them over and over again. He is a wonderfully forgiving Father.
- We learn to practice a forgiving spirit and be willing to apologize and ask forgiveness when we have offended someone else.

Father,

We are so glad that prayer does not depend on being completely sinless — if that were the case, no one could ever pray. You tell us to confess our sin and ask forgiveness. But our willingness to forgive others is a vital part of the prayer equation, too.

There are times, Father, when we want to hang onto certain sins; we like to come to You in prayer and pretend they don't exist. But Your Holy Spirit doesn't allow that. He brings them to our attention. The Spirit is usually gentle but is relentless about the sins we won't relinquish. We're so glad He doesn't dump on us, overwhelming us. The Spirit deals with one issue at a time. Help us to respond to His conviction by repenting and forsaking whatever He brings to our mind as we pray. And help us to forgive others.

Day 8

And lead us not into temptation
but deliver us from the evil one.
— Matthew 6:13

If you are perplexed by the first half of this text, you are not alone. Many believers have questions about it. At first glance, it seems possible that God tempts us, and we should be asking Him not to do that. Is it true that God tempts us? No! James 1:13 says God can't be tempted by evil and He doesn't tempt anyone else, either. Then, what is Christ talking about when He instructs us to pray, asking that we not to be led into temptation — what does He mean by that?

Matt. 6:13 is what we could call the **protection aspect** of prayer. Satan is a "roaring lion" (1 Pet. 5:8) and is continually battling against believers. He is a liar, a deceiver, a manipulator, a murderer, and a destroyer. The second half of Matt. 6:13 instructs us to ask protection from Satan. We don't have too much trouble understanding this last part of the verse.

But the first half — about not leading us into temptation — might need some clarification. Two other Scriptures help us understand.

One is an incident in Matt. 26:41, which is the account where Christ is praying in the garden of Gethsemane just prior to His arrest and crucifixion. Jesus is in agonizing prayer, but the disciples keep falling asleep.

They have no clue as to what the next several hours will bring. Jesus wakes them up. He tells them, "Watch and pray so that You will not fall into temptation. The spirit is willing, but the flesh is weak" (Matt. 26:41). Christ is telling them they should be praying for protection from the evil one (as He instructed them in the model prayer) so that they don't yield to temptation; that is, that they don't yield to their own weaknesses in the trying events that are about to come. It's possible that if Peter had been praying for protection, he might not have denied Christ three times.

The second Scripture that helps us understand Matt. 6:13a is in 1 Cor. 10:13:

> *No temptation has seized You except what is common to man. And God is faithful; he will not let You be tempted beyond what You can bear. But when You are tempted, he will also provide a way out so that You can stand up under it.*

It helps us to know that 1 Cor. 10:13 is a parallel to Matt. 6:13a, but in the form of a promise. It's the same concept, clarified and said in a different way. It is a promise that assures us of God's help in the middle of extreme temptation and His provision of a way out. So ...

Matt. 6:13 is the *instruction to pray for protection from the evil one.*

Matt. 26:41 is an *illustration of a time when this aspect of prayer was needed.*

And 1 Cor. 10:13 is the *promise of God's answer when we ask protection.*

Praying according to Matt. 6:13a is petitioning God not to leave us unattended, without help, in the temptations where we are most vulnerable. We are asking for the way out He has promised and protection from the lies, the deception, the manipulation, and the destruction of Satan himself. It's impossible to pray for God's protection too often, because the evil one attacks when we are the most vulnerable.

Let's pray for ourselves and the world-wide Church that:

- The LORD will deliver us from the attacks of evil.
- He will provide us a way out from temptation.

Father,

You know our particular weaknesses. We seem to be asking forgiveness in the same areas over and over again. Would You especially guard us in these areas and deliver us?

Day 9

*Dear friends, if our hearts do not condemn
us, we have confidence before God.*
— Matthew 6:21

Before we leave the model prayer completely, let's consider one more verse that has close connection to it. First John 3:21-22 indicates that if we are not convicted in our hearts when we pray, we can have confidence in God's hearing us.

Every believer commits a great deal of sin every day. Some we are not even aware of. But in the sanctification process, God treats us like immature, but beloved children. He patiently walks along with us, points out things that are wrong, corrects us, forgives us, welcomes us back in His arms, and moves on. He considers that we are dust and deals with us in a manner consistent with our maturity. There's lots of conviction from the Holy Spirit, lots of reassurances of His love, lots of further instruction when we are ignorant. He sees we are not willful rebels — just children in need of wise, Fatherly discipline and training.

But the privilege of God granting us a blank check to ask Him for anything in prayer is another matter. It does not co-exist with stubborn refusal to confess and repent when the Holy Spirit brings something to our attention during prayer. It's like the son that's been promised a trip to the sports store as soon as school is over, but when he gets home

26

— bouncing into the house expecting the promise to be fulfilled — the parent informs him they discovered something that had been left undone when he left for school. The son's room was a complete mess. Clothes were all over the floor, the bed wasn't made, and fast-food containers were tossed here and there. There were clear household rules concerning these things and they had been violated.

This neglect is not a matter of patient parental training. This is nose-to-nose confrontation. The parent has every intention of keeping the promise — the trip is a sure thing. But the mess must be taken care of *now. There's not going to be one step taken toward the sports store until the clothes are off the floor, the bed is made, and the trash is put where it belongs.* Disobedience has hindered the completion of the promise.

There are many *now* issues that God insists we deal with when we pray; but lack of forgiveness is a very frequent one. It's something God wants taken care of immediately, and He seems to push the pause button on answered prayer until we resolve it. Besides that, unforgiveness and grudges are very heavy loads to carry. They put us in bondage. As the saying goes, harboring unforgiveness is like drinking poison and expecting it to affect someone else. If we want God to forgive the offenses that are hindering our prayer, we are going to have to forgive the offenses others have committed against us.

Let's pray that we have tender hearts in responding to the conviction of the Holy Spirit when we come to the LORD in prayer — especially if we need to forgive.

Father,
As hard as it is to forgive when we feel we are justified in it, there is no sin worth harboring if it obstructs prayer. You have

forgiven us mountains of sin — so shouldn't we forgive the anthill of wrong someone else has committed against us? Help us to humble ourselves and ask forgiveness of others when we wrong them — and forgive those who wrong us.

Day 10

In the same way, the Spirit helps us in our weakness.
We do not know what we ought to pray for, but the
Spirit himself intercedes for us through wordless
groans. And he who searches our hearts knows the
mind of the Spirit, because the Spirit intercedes for
God's people in accordance with the will of God.
— Romans 8:26-27

Once when our youngest daughter was around 3 years old, I left her with her father for the afternoon. I returned several hours later to a very puzzled husband. "She keeps asking me for something," he said, "but I have no idea what she's talking about. She wants a 'going-up seat.' Do you know what she wants?"

I laughed, because as the one who spent hours with this little girl and understood the desires of her heart, I knew exactly what she meant. I explained it to him, and the next Saturday, her father went to the hardware and came home with a sturdy 2x8, some chains, some big eyebolts, and a little red plastic seat. He got his ladder, climbed up the trunks of a couple of trees, and built her a swing.

As one who understands us completely, God the Holy Spirit is critically involved when we pray. He performs one of His several ministries in us as He takes our prayer to God, makes spiritual sense of it, and conforms it to God's will. What we struggle to express, He knows completely and makes known to the Father.

It's important we understand this collaboration between God the Holy Spirit and God the Father. We often feel our prayer is inadequate. Our understanding of the people and situations we are praying for is very limited. We often can't see the root of the problems, so of course we can't see their solutions. We don't know what to ask for; but God the Father who searches our hearts — and the hearts of those we're praying for — knows the mind of the Spirit. And the Holy Spirit understands us as He intercedes, conforming our prayer to the will of God.

Our knowledge about the Spirit's role in prayer may not yet be complete, but we know this: We are dependent on the Holy Spirit for His help, and we should look to Him and trust Him to effectively express to God the Father what we cannot.

Let's pray that we not fret about what we think is inadequate prayer, but trust in the interceding work of the Holy Spirit to make spiritual sense of what we ask, as we look to Him.

Father,

You know our thoughts before we even think them, and our words before we ever speak them. Thank You that Your Spirit, who indwells us, intercedes with perfect understanding about those things we can't even put into words. You hear the very cry of our hearts and respond according to Your will. Thank You, Father.

Day 11

All Scripture is God-breathed ... .
— *2 Timothy 3:16a*

Back in the days before cell phones, I remember eating alone in a restaurant and being intrigued with a middle-aged couple who came in and sat opposite me. They were obviously married — both had on wedding rings, but they gained my attention because they never said a word to each other. They looked at the menu and ordered when the waitress came, but then, with a bored expression, she gazed out the window and he watched some sporting event on television. This went on through the entire meal. When I left, I glanced back at them. There was only a table between them, but they were still locked in isolated silence. I don't know which one I felt the sorrier for. If this dinner hour was typical of their marriage, they were two miserably isolated people.

Our relationship with God is not like that couple's relationship to one another. In the first few verses of the Bible — and all the way through — we find God speaking. All Scripture is "breathed" out from Him. In other words, God speaks, and believers are given the incredible opportunity to respond to Him. The very essence of prayer consists of a response to the speaking God. We would not even know of a supreme being to address had not God first placed us in His amazing creation and then introduced Himself to us in His Word. He is the initiator. He starts the conversing.

One of the greatest joys in prayer is the dialoguing back and forth with God as we read his Word. As He reveals things about Himself, about us, about the world we live in and where it came from; about what the future holds, about what is eternally valuable and what is not, we are offered the ultimate relationship — to discuss all things with Almighty God.

We could be reading Isaiah 52 — and right in the middle of it, tell the LORD, "I get it! You're talking prophetically about the crucifixion of Jesus in verses 13-15."

We could read a section in Matt. 3:11-12 and say to Him, "I think I understand being baptized with the Holy Spirit — but what are You talking about in being baptized with fire? Would You help me understand what that means?" It's exciting to see Him answer us when we pray like this.

Let's read Scripture the same way a prospector looks for gold...expectant, excited, motivated, dedicated and cognizant of the worth; because when we respond to God as we read and dialogue with Him, we will see His hand in our lives.

Reading the Bible does not lead us to an encounter with God — it IS an encounter with God.

— Henry Blackaby

Father,

Help us to comprehend that when we read Scripture, we have opportunity to interact with You. Thank You for speaking to us Spirit-to-spirit, face-to-face: in a sense, up close and personal.

Help us to take great care how we respond to You. May we not have hardened hearts that are indifferent and unbelieving; or cold and distracted. But may we have soft, hungering hearts that long for You and desire to know You. May we be transparent and completely honest — because You know our thoughts before they ever come into our mind, and our reactions before they are apparent.

Father, we understand that any relationship demands give-and-take communication. Without it, no real relationship can exist. We would be always second-guessing intention, misunderstanding actions, and suspicious of intimacy. But when we know all Scripture is Your Word to us, and You want response from us, there is mutual understanding. Father, may we read Your Word — and respond to it — as if we were mining gold and precious gems; for in the spiritual economy, that's exactly what we are doing.

Day 12

I love the LORD, for he heard my voice;
he heard my cry for mercy.
Because he turned his ear to me,
I will call on him as long as I live.
— Psalm 116:1-2

How do we view prayer?

How we view prayer enormously affects the quality of our prayer life. If we view it as something we would like to do, but just have no time for, we won't find the time. If we view it as boring and difficult, we will avoid it. If we view it as a tiresome duty, we will resent it. If we view it as something that—to be honest, seems to have little effect on how things really work out — we will carry a hidden feeling of disappointment and disillusionment. If we view it as something only super-saints practice, we will feel inadequate.

If we view it as only a means of trying to talk a reluctant God into paying attention and doing something about all our personal problems and desires — we'll miss the power source that God intends prayer to be.

While we may at times feel we never have time to pray, it's not really a matter of time: It's a matter of priority. It's possible to develop the attitude, "If I don't get anything else done in a day, I need to pray. I really, really need to pray."

Prayer loses the perception of being boring and difficult when we realize it is the lifeline between us and headquarters — it is the center for communication and supply. More and more we realize it is not a tiresome duty — it is a delightful response to God as we commune with Him while reading or contemplating His Word.

Prayer is not ineffective! It is the means of power for ministry and life.

We don't have to be super-saints to pray — small children can talk to the Father. The newest believer can approach the throne of the living God and pour out his or her heart to Him. It's not about approaching a reluctant God and trying to talk Him into doing something about our personal needs — it is the means of "cast[ing] all Your anxiety on him because he cares for You" (1 Pet. 5:7) and finding peace the world can't understand.

We must not kid ourselves: The spiritual health and vitality of any church (and the individual believer, as well) is directly proportional to the health and vitality of the prayer life. Just as the pulse is a vital sign for physical life, a healthy prayer life is one of the vital signs in spiritual life. It's the undeniable evidence of a living, functioning relationship with the Triune God.

Let's pray for the world-wide Church, our own congregation, our pastor(s), our leaders, our teachers, and ourselves that:

- We view prayer as a priority in our lives; that we see what a lifeline it is for believers.
- We view prayer as the source of power for life and ministry.
- We view prayer as the place where we can pour out our souls to God and cast our cares on Him.
- We understand God is not reluctant to hear us; on the contrary, He stoops to listen as we pray.

Father,

It is so easy to get up in the morning and have the affairs of life demand our immediate attention. But if we allow these demands to monopolize our attention, and do not give time with You our first priority, these daily affairs will starve our relationship with You.

Father, we desperately need You to hear our prayers! We desperately need to be listening and responding to You! If we want You to listen to us, we must be listening — really listening — to You.

Day 13

And when you pray, do not keep on babbling
like pagans, for they think they will be heard
because of their many words.
— Matthew 6:7

Heaven forbid that the Church pray babbling, pagan-like prayer. We should be practicing prayer that is the exact polar opposite — but what would that look like?

Charles Spurgeon, often called the "Prince of Preachers," wrote:

> True prayer is measured **by weight, not by length**.
> A single groan may have more fullness of prayer in it
> than a fine oration of great length. [emphasis added]

What did he mean by this? What makes prayer heavy? Here is an illustration:

A father is approached by his two sons who both want to borrow the car at the same time. The father asks the usual questions — Where are you going? Why do you need it? Who is going with you? What time will you be back? Do you have money for gas?

Son #1 wants to go to the beach with his friends. He spent his money on other things, so has nothing left for gas. His room is a wreck, even though he has been instructed to clean it twice. He has teased and fought with his sister incessantly, left his chores undone and made a rude remark about a meal his mother served.

Son #2 wants to drive to an adjoining city to take his SAT test so he can meet the deadline for college applications. His room, although not perfect, at least contains a visible bed and does not have small animals living in the debris. He expressed appreciation to his mother over a small favor, and his laundry is done. He studied hard for finals and kept up with his jobs around the house. The week before, when he borrowed the car, he was home on time.

Which son do You think the father would judge to have the **weightier request**?

This illustration, although not perfect, gives some idea of what Spurgeon meant when he referred to "heavy" prayer. God has a criterion for what He judges heavy prayer. Heavy prayer has underlying obedience in it. Heavy prayer recognizes who and what God is and expresses thankfulness to Him. It is prayer that is sold out to God and His purposes. It submits to God's will even as it cries out to Him in difficult circumstances. Heavy prayer exhibits humility.

— Praise and worship are components of heavy prayer.
— Longing for God and loving Him deeply are components of heavy prayer.
— Prayer in line with God's Word is a component of heavy prayer — unquestionably.
— Faith is always an essential component.

Our churches, our world, and our people need **heavy prayer**.

Please pray for the world-wide Church, our own congregation, our own pastor(s), our leaders, our teachers, and ourselves, that we pray prayers that are:

- The exact opposite of pagan prayer.
- Heavy with honesty and candor and humility.
- Weighty with longing for His Kingdom to come and His will to be done on earth.
- HEAVY with faith — firmly convinced that God hears and answers.
- Weighty with praise, worship and thanksgiving.

Day 14

One day Jesus was praying in a certain place.
When he finished, one of his disciples said to him,
"Lord, teach us to pray, just as John taught his disciples."
— Luke 1:11

One of the most glorious aspects of prayer is that it is a private sanctuary where we withdraw from the confusing turmoil of this present world, shut the door, and find everything we need for the challenges of life from the hand of our Father. The disciple in Luke 1:11 must have seen what prayer meant to Jesus, and he wanted the same intimate relationship with God.

But like everything else, there is a learning curve involved. Prayer is a spiritual skill just as playing a piano, or riding a bicycle, or ice skating, or carpentry work are physical skills. We learn from the simplest principles and build on them. We learn new concepts about prayer, practice them, master them, and become skillful. How encouraging to both us and the LORD, the whole learning process is satisfying and delightful. God inclines His ear to both the beginner and the proficient.

We learn to pray by sitting down and applying ourselves to its practice, even though we may not know everything about it. But at the same time, there's a need to follow the examples and principles found throughout the Bible. For instance, God responds to honesty and a submissive spirit rather than trite phrases; to a teachable spirit rather than stubborn resistance; to true heart-affected response to His Word rather than lip service; to longing for interaction with Him rather than hurried indifference; to delight in His presence rather than dry duty.

There are dozens of examples where God's people pray throughout Scripture. We learn discipline in prayer from Daniel (Dan. 6:10). We learn worship in prayer from Isaiah (Is. 25:1). We learn to pour out our hearts with our inner-most sorrows to God from David and the other psalmists.

Christ teaches us that prayer should be persistent in Matt. 7:7-11. We observe impactful prayer as Hannah prays (1 Sam. chapters 1 and 2). We learn desperate prayer from Hezekiah (Is. 37:14-20). Christ shows us the efficacy of repentant prayer, rather than proud religion, in the prayer of the Pharisee and the sinner (Luke 18:9-14). We learn the balm of heart-broken prayer as Jeremiah weeps over Jerusalem (Lam. 5). We are shown beautiful acceptance of God's will and simple trust from Mary (Luke 1:38). We see the power available to us in prayer from the believers in the first few chapters of Acts.

May we be eager students of prayer. May we ignore the setbacks and things we don't understand and pray as trusting — even though sometimes confused and tripping — children of our Father.

Let's pray for the Church — that we keep on trying, even when we don't think we know very much about effective prayer.

Father,

We fail You in many ways; but when we stand before You and our works are judged on whether they are gold or whether they are straw, we want one thing to be true about us — that we have honestly sought Your face in prayer. And help us to search the Scriptures eagerly and diligently to see how You instruct us on it.

Day 15

When you ask, you do not receive, because
you ask with wrong motives, that you may
spend what you get on your pleasures.
— James 4:3

Just before a great orchestra comes together to play, all the different instruments must be tuned to each other. An "A" is sounded, and all orchestra members adjust their instruments to that pitch. Only when this is successfully completed is it possible for the flutes, the violins, the cellos, the brass etc., to bring their unique sounds together — not in individual discord, but in united beauty and harmony.

Writing on this topic in his classic, *The Pursuit of God*, A.W. Tozer said, "Has it ever occurred to you that 100 pianos all tuned to the same fork [pitch] are automatically tuned to each other?" He is making an analogy between musical instruments and the churches of Christ. Just as an orchestra must have a musical standard all the musicians submit their instruments to, so the members of Christ — if there is to be unity — must be submitted to the single spiritual standard of Christlikeness. It does no good to try and keep eliminating controversial things in order to reach the least common denominator of opinions. This is as impossible a goal as each musician in an orchestra attempting to quit playing all notes not in tune with the tuning fork. It's unattainable.

If all people insist on having what they want all the time in all matters, eternity together is impossible. Without unity and submission to God, human beings simply cannot live together for any length of time, let alone eternity.

One of the reasons God leaves us on this earth after the salvation experience is to bring us through all the knotholes of life that teach conformity to Jesus Christ. Not satisfied with just theological theory, God insists on practical application. We must actually learn to live out unity with the Triune God.

Prayer, by its very nature, demands this unity with God. If we are to pray according to His will — it calls for us to "tune" to Him. We accomplish this principle when we are careful to align our prayer with the Scriptures.

The world waits to see the reality of Christ being proved out in the lives of its adherents. It is watching for people who are Christ-like in character. It is not satisfied with promises, promises: The world wants to see — needs to see — is dying to see — authentic Christians living out authentic Christlikeness, the fruit of a living relationship with God.

The Church wants to see — needs to see — and is dying to see believers who pray, not so that they can get what they want for their own pleasure, but because they *want what God wants.*

Let's pray for the world-wide Church that we be "tuned" to the standard of Jesus in our words, our actions, our motives, our values, our purposes; and most critical of all — in our prayers.

Father,

    We realize You are not a genie in a bottle that we use to get what we want. You are the Great I AM, the only one wise enough, strong enough, far-seeing enough, loving enough, just enough, and immutable enough to rule all things. We don't want to try and use You — we want to be Yours to use.

Day 16

————— *Do not conform any longer to the pattern of this* —————
world, but be transformed by the renewing of your
mind. Then you will be able to test and approve what
God's will is — his good, pleasing and perfect will.
— Romans 12:2

I once knew an earnest Christian couple faced with two job offers at the same time. They fretted over which one was God's will for them. They knew this one decision would have far-reaching effect on their family and they wanted to be located where God wanted them. Like so many believers, they struggled with how to determine God's will. How do we know which guy or girl to marry? Where should we live? Should we buy the used Buick or the new Toyota?

God doesn't spell out His will regarding such details of life. He gives us wisdom principles by which we must make decisions about them. But Romans 12:2 says a renewed mind that's been transformed by God's instruction in Scripture can discern His will *about things that He does spell out.* Andrew Murray, in his book, *God's Will: Our Dwelling Place,* looks at the whole of Scripture and distills from it four ways God reveals His will to His children[1]:

---

1 Excerpts and quotes from *God's Will: Our Dwelling Place* by Andrew Murray, copyright 1982 by Whitaker House. Published by Whitaker House, New Kensington, PA. Used by permission. All rights reserved. www.whitakerhouse.com.

First, God reveals His will through His **providence**. Murray writes, "Everything that happens on earth comes to the child of God as the will of the Father." We usually see this as the common blessings we enjoy — food, shelter, income, etc. But it also includes things we don't consider so positive — things we don't like but we can't remove. The good and the bad both come to us within the sovereign providence of God. **We do God's will when we accept all things in our lives as from the loving hand of God.** Murray writes:

> When the Christian learns to see everything that happens to him — grievous or pleasing, great or small — the prayer, *Thy will be done,* will become the unceasing expression of adoring submission and praise. The whole world with its dark mysteries, life, and difficulties, will be illuminated by the light of God's presence and rule. The soul will taste the rest and the bliss of knowing that it is always encircled and watched over by God's will. ... Happy is the Christian who receives everything in providence as the will of His Father.

Second, God reveals His will through His **precepts**. Precepts are clear, black and white instructions God gives us in His Word on how to live. "Do to others as You would have them do to You" (Luke 6:31) is a precept. So is "Be devoted to one another in love" (Romans 12:10). **We do God's will when we — yielding to the conviction of the Holy Spirit — obey the precepts.**

Third, God reveals His will in His **promises**. All through Scripture, in both the Old Testament and the New, we see God promising to do something IF we will do something. We're told, "Resist the devil and he will flee from You" (James 4:7 KJV). "Come unto me ... and I will give You rest" (Matt. 11:28 KJV). "Delight thyself also in the Lord: and he shall give thee the desires of thine heart" (Ps. 37:4 KJV). **We do His will when we believe His promises and step out in obedience to the conditions.**

Fourth, God reveals His will in His **purposes.** Christians are involved in the events of this world where God sovereignly moves events toward the consummation of His perfect, eternal plan. Daniel was caught in God' purposes when he was taken in the Babylonian captivity; Joseph's life was forever impacted when he was taken to Egypt as a slave. Mary faced social disgrace when she submitted to being the mother of Jesus. When we see things happening on a much bigger stage than our own lives, things we can't do anything about, we are part of God's bringing about His purposes. How do we do His will in these instances? **We do God's will in His purposes when we patiently persevere.**

Let's pray for ourselves and the Church that we accept all things in life — the good and the bad — as His loving providence; that we obey His precepts; that we trust and step out on His promises; and that we patiently persevere in His purposes.

Day 17

Remember the former things, those of long ago.
I am God, and there is no other;
I am God, and there is none like me.
I make known the end from the beginning,
from ancient times, what is still to come.
I say, 'My purpose will stand,
and I will do all that I please.'
— Isaiah 46:9-10

We have a Heavenly Father who has a big-picture plan. It encompasses everything from the creation in Genesis 1 to the consummation of all things in Revelation 22:21. The LORD knows what He is doing and where He is going. He's not side-tracked by the ups and downs of human endeavors. He has already determined the end from way back at the beginning, and our lives are a component of this God-sized epic.

But at the same time, He is a loving Father who understands the frailties of His children. He walks hand-in-hand with them — not just in the demands of His eternal plans and purposes, but also in the challenges of their personal lives while they must contend in an imperfect world.

One of our challenges as intercessors/petitioners is to not fall off the horse on either side when it comes to these two extremes. We pray not just for God's big-picture plans, but also about the pain and difficulties all believers, ourselves included, encounter right now in this present physical existence. We should pray fervently toward both ends, not neglecting one to concentrate on the other.

Our interaction with God is a learning curve we will be on until the day He takes us home. Until that day comes, our interaction with Him will be like a small child who trails after his father on a camping trip. Sometimes they will discuss such practical things as the problem the child has getting the tent pegs pounded in the ground; and sometimes they will talk about the father's impending mission trip where he will be involved in making disciples on the other side of the world.

Many of the lessons the father teaches are absorbed during the process, rather than memorized by rote lecture. For example, the father can be counted on to know the right direction to drive; the father provides the fire, the matches, and the food (to which the child never gave a thought at the beginning of the trip). The car, the gasoline, the tent all seem to appear out of nowhere. The child trails along in complete confidence, even though he has no idea where the path will lead. At the end of the day, the little one lies down in a foreign environment and sleeps peacefully — secure in the father's presence. In the same way, there is companionship, trust, instruction, enjoyment, love, and honest communication between the Father and us in prayer. We are free to address both topics in prayer — present needs and God's eternal plans.

Let's pray that we realize we pray on two fronts simultaneously — for the fulfillment of God's plans and purposes, and, also, for the practical needs and situations His children face every day.

Father,

We think of Your purposes and plans as somehow being distinctly separate from the details of what is happening to us — Your children — right now in this present world; but they are not! Help us to realize that our present needs and Your eternal plans are actually intertwined. Help us to see that what we learn in the trials of life and in our relationship to You in prayer IS part of Your eternal plans and purposes to advance Christ's Kingdom along. Help us to keep our eyes on You and enjoy the trip as we see Your purposes unfold. Help us to relax by just being in Your presence, and hear our prayers, we ask. Amen.

Day 18

My prayer is not for them alone. I pray also for those who will believe in me through their message, that all of them may be one, Father, just as you are in me and I am in you. May they also be in us so that the world may believe that you have sent me.
— John 17:20-21

It is welcome words when anyone tells us they are praying for us, because enlisting God's help amid our dilemmas is the very best help they can give us. But how much infinitely greater and more magnificent is the fact that *Jesus* prayed for us!

Right before His arrest and crucifixion, Christ prayed the Great High Priestly prayer recorded in John 17:1-26. Among His requests in this passage, Jesus petitions God for something beyond mind-boggling. He asks that New Testament believers be in an intimate relationship of one-ness with the Triune Godhead. Since the coming of the Holy Spirit at Pentecost and His indwelling of believers, this prayer has been answered and is indeed true. *It is a present tense, positional, spiritual reality for believers of this age.*

It helps us understand prayer when we understand there are *five passages that make up the bedrock on which God's plan for prayer, in our time, is built.*

The **first passage** is our text, John 17:20-21. It is the relationship factor:

> *"My prayer is not for them alone. I pray also for those who will believe in me through their message, that all of them may be one, Father, just as You are in me and I am in You. May they also be in us so that the world may believe that You have sent me.*

The **second passage** is Rom. 8:9 — the Holy Spirit indwelling believers factor:

> *You, however, are controlled not by the sinful nature but by the Spirit, if the Spirit of God lives in You. And if anyone does not have the Spirit of Christ, he does not belong to Christ.*

The **third passage** is Eph. 1:19-20 — the Christ seated at God's right-hand factor:

> *... and his incomparably great power for us who believe. That power is like the working of his mighty strength, which he exerted in Christ when he raised him from the dead and seated him at his right hand in the heavenly realms ...*

The **fourth passage** is Rom. 8:34 — the Christ continually interceding factor:

> *Who is he that condemns? Christ Jesus who died — more than that, who was raised to life — is at the right hand of God and is also interceding for us.*

And the **fifth passage** is Eph. 2:5-6 ASV — we sit with/in Christ in the heavenlies factor:

> *... even when we were dead through our trespasses, made us alive together with Christ (by grace have ye been saved), and raised us up with him, and made us to sit with him in the heavenly places, in Christ Jesus.*

So, we can succinctly sum up the relationship bedrock on which prayer in this age is built:

- Believers are in a united (at-one-with) relationship with all three members of the Trinity.
- The Holy Spirit of God indwells the believer.
- Christ is right now seated at God's right hand in the heavenly realm.
- Christ continually makes intercession for us.
- And — *what a wonder!* — we are seated with Him and invited, commanded even — to come to the Throne of Grace and offer up all kinds of prayer in connection to, and in Him (Eph. 6:18).

Whether we are aware of it or not, all New Testament prayer is possible because of this living relationship with the Godhead. We do not pray alone. On one hand, we pray in unity with Christ our Great High Priest and Advocate; and on the other hand, we pray in unity with the Holy Spirit who motivates, leads, enables, and conforms our prayer to the will of God. All these interactions work together as we address the Father in prayer.

Let's pray for all God's people and ourselves that:

We be enormously encouraged, and more than a little bit awed, by the fact that Christ Himself and the Holy Spirit participate with us in real prayer and present it to the Father. May we grasp what this relationship means to our prayer life; and may we marvel at the privilege and possibilities it affords.

Father,

We are incredibly encouraged and delighted by the bedrock of prayer that Jesus purchased for us.

*As believers, we need not worry that our prayers are spoken out into a void — as if we sit huddled in a dark corner, not knowing if You hear us or not. Father, You have assured us of Your **presence** in an utterly complete way. There is intimacy, warmth, comradery and security in this, the most sacred relationship people can ever be privileged to be a part of.*

Certainly, let us marvel at the privilege and possibilities this relationship affords.

Day 19

My prayer is not for them alone. I pray also for
those who will believe in me through their message.
— John 17:20

When we see death approaching, we don't talk to our loved ones about trivial and inconsequential things. Instead, we address significant and vital information we want them always to remember. The seriousness of our words is engraved with the seriousness of our own departure. The last words of the dying have always been treasured by those who love them.

Believers, too, have always treasured the High Priestly Prayer of Jesus in John 17:1-26, because His prayer was filled with significant and vital information for us even as He faced an agonizing death. His prayer addressed deep, doctrinal issues. It encompassed things starting from God's eternal decrees — to the final destiny of His followers — to the glory Christ will have at the consummation of all things.

These intercessions in John 17 are not little things! We addressed one of them — Christ asking for a unity of oneness with Himself, the Father, and other believers — in a previous entry; but there are at least 7 others. Jesus was betrayed, arrested, unjustly accused, tortured, and finally crucified to obtain them for us. Should we not fervently desire what He asked for? Should we not, if we are seeking to be praying according to God's will, join Him in asking these same requests for His church?

Jesus asked:

1. Glorify me so I can glorify You (v. 1).
2. Shield believers by Your name (v. 11).
3. Shield believers from Satan (v. 15).
4. Set apart believers to Yourself (v. 17).
5. Give believers unity with the Father and the Son, in the same way the Father is in Christ and Christ is in the Father (vs. 21-23).
6. Allow believers to be with Jesus so they can see His glorious worth (v. 24).
7. Allow me to continue showing them that the love You have always had for me can be in them, too (v. 26).

Praying for the same things Christ prayed in John 17 is a high and holy form of prayer indeed. When we pray these same requests, our perspective is lifted as high as the Godhead. Our fellowship with Christ is made sweet, intense, and as focused as a laser beam because we are united with Him in those things dearest to His heart.

Let's pray for the world-wide Church that God would glorify Himself and Jesus Christ. That:

- God would protect us by His powerful name.
- He would shield us from the evil one.
- He would set us apart by His Word — and with extreme patience.
- We might realize our unity with the Triune God.
- We would look forward to, pray for, and wait for the day we will actually be with the Lord forever.
- We would see more and more of God's glory — His infinite worth — and the same love God the Father has for Jesus would be realized in us and lived out in practical ways toward others.
- We would realize these requests are the heart-desires of Jesus.

Father,

You have created us with the capacity for emotions that range from the very simple all the way to the very sublime. This prayer of Jesus — spoken so closely to the crucifixion — is surely the greatest prayer ever offered. It expresses in very simple words the highest privileges human beings can ever attain, and it stirs our emotions ineffably. How can we express how we feel?

You protect us, You shield us from the evil one, and You set us apart for Yourself. You not only give us the privilege of being with You for all eternity; but You place us in Your inner circle — to enjoy the love and fellowship You have had between the members of the Godhead since eternity past. And this privilege is not just for heaven but is given to us right now! What a wonder!

Help us to understand it all and enable us to pray so that the concepts of this prayer are bestowed on all believers we know ... and to Your Church all over the world.

We long for the day when we see Jesus come in power and great glory. But until that day comes, please give us the grace and faith to continue following hard after You. Amen.

Day 20

*"God is spirit, and his worshipers must
worship in spirit and in truth."*
— John 4:24

God does not want dry, apathetic, sterile relationships with His children. He wants our hearts. He wants us to be in love with and captivated with Him. He wants us to truly worship — that is, have our minds, our emotions, our will — our spirit! — centered on the worth-ship of the Triune God. He wants our prayer to be saturated with these attitudes.

Here is what some other godly men have said about genuine worship:

> "Some of the most rapturous moments we know will be those we spend in reverent admiration of the Godhead. In those holy moments the very thought of change in Him will be too painful to endure."
>
> — A.W. Tozer

> "Missions is not the ultimate goal of the church. Worship is. Missions exist because worship doesn't."
>
> — John Piper

"Worship and intercession go together; one is impossible
without the other."
— Oswald Chambers

It seems that someday, when we are in the glorified state, prayer as we
presently know it will end. But worship will never cease. We will spend
eternity learning about, admiring, rejoicing in, wondering at, and having
loving relationship with the Great I AM. We will never get enough of
Him.

Worship does something wonderful for the believer — in it we are
giving evidence that we really believe what we are saying about the LORD,
and we are opening our hearts to experience the reality of it. We recognize
God as the real and ultimate solution to all our needs. When we worship
Him as Righteous Judge, for instance, we know that someday, all wrongs
will be made right. If we worship Him as Jehovah-Jireh, our provider,
we don't fret about the needs of life. When we worship Christ as LORD
of all lords and King of all kings, the shifting sands of political upheaval
lose their power to terrify. Worship is the best tonic for the dark pit of
discouragement and depression. It is the "only reasonable response to
God's revelation of Himself" (unknown). It's a never-ending delight to
daily find newer and bigger and richer topics of worship.

Let's pray for ourselves and believers everywhere that:

- We would be captivated by our admiration of the Lord.
- Worship would bubble up out of our spirits like cool refreshing springs as we read what God reveals of Himself in Scripture.
- When we worship, our hearts will be calmed and secure like the "weaned child" of Ps. 131:2.

Father,

We are made in Your image — and we certainly don't want a dry, apathetic, uninvolved relationship either. We want real, warm, intimate, interaction with You. May worship spring from every part of our being — our emotions, our intellect, our will, and our passion. May we honestly see You as You reveal Yourself in Scripture and experience You as it describes.

Day 21

*But when you pray, go into your room, close
the door and pray to your Father, who is
unseen. Then your Father, who sees
what is done in secret, will reward you.*

— *Matthew 6:6*

Is it important for us to have a regular, disciplined, secret prayer life? Yes, it is. This verse seems to assume that we regularly pray, and it gives instructions for how to go about it. It is to be spoken to our Father in intimate secrecy. Although it's possible (even desirable) to pray while driving a car or engaging in other activities during the day, spur-of-the-moment prayer does not and cannot replace the focused, disciplined, set-apart time that Jesus is talking about here in Matt. 6:6.

Spurgeon wrote:

> "There is no doubt that it is by praying that we learn to pray, and that the more we pray, the better our prayers will be. People who pray in spurts are never likely to attain the kind of prayer described in the Scriptures as 'powerful and effective ...'" (James 5:16).

Prayer that is rich in praise and worship, heavy with faith in what

God's Word says, burdened for His church, feverish for what only God can do for a dying world, and centered on His Kingdom purposes is not the product of an impulsive moment. It is prayer of a considered, biblically driven purpose, with an urgency about it that demands time and priority.

We would never even consider appearing for an appointment with our boss at work in an unprepared manner. We would want the facts and figures they need, the paperwork printed and in order, input from several of our own subordinates, and thought-out requests that benefit the company — all gathered before we walk through the door. How much more should our hearts be prepared to bring before God the most pressing needs of those around us. How much more should we be entirely focused on meeting with Him, not distracted by interruptions and other demands. How much more should we realize the importance of regularly meeting with Him.

Regular, disciplined, secret prayer provides a springboard from which "spurts" of prayer can rise naturally throughout the day; but is not true the other way around. Spurts of prayer very seldom give rise to regular, disciplined, secret prayer. Christ instructs us to go into a room, shut the door, and pray to our Father in secret — then we are given a conditional promise. When we do as He instructs, our Father "who sees what is done in secret" (Matt. 6:6) will reward us.

Please pray for the world-wide Church, that:

- We would, like Daniel, be people of regular, disciplined, secret prayer.
- We would treasure and delight in this time between the Triune God and ourselves.
- We would see God wonderfully reward secret prayer — not just in eternity, but in seeing changes in the circumstances of the here and now.

Father,

We have found the joy of secret, disciplined prayer to be exactly what we need for each day. Without it, our souls are left hungering and thirsty. Father, let us build our plans for the day around the need for this sweet communion with You. Let us discipline ourselves to get out of bed earlier and find a place where nobody can interrupt us — and help us leave the phones out of the picture. We ask You to protect us from intrusions. After all, this is our lifeline!

Day 22

One day Jesus was praying in a certain
place. When he finished, one of his
disciples said to him, "Lord, teach us
to pray, just as John taught his disciples."
— Luke 11:1

Over 300 years ago a poor man of common education and background was arrested for preaching without a license, charges brought from the Church of England. He sat in a cold British jail and began to write what would become a classic in Christian literature. John Bunyan's *Pilgrim's Progress* would influence believers for generations. Among his other writings is an insightful definition of prayer.

> Prayer is a sincere, sensible, affectionate pouring out of
> the heart or soul to God through Christ, in the strength
> and assistance of the Holy Spirit, for such things as God
> has promised, or according to His Word, for the good of
> the church with submission in faith.
> — John Bunyan 1628-1688

Like a beautifully cut diamond, prayer has many facets and can be described in hundreds of ways. But if we were to take everything Scripture says about prayer, distill it down to its essential elements, and write it in succinct poetry, we would have a hard time improving on Bunyan's definition. The only thing we might think is missing is the instruction to pray for all people, not just the Church; but it's not missing. Bunyan says to pray according to God's Word, and 1 Tim. 2:1-3 makes it clear we are to pray for all people.

Christ's model prayer in Matt. 6:9-13 teaches us who we pray to and what to pray for: It covers all our real needs. But Bunyan's definition looks at the whole of Scripture and teaches us the major structure and character of prayer: its essential elements, process, scope, and focus.

Just as God used men like Wycliffe and Tyndale to translate the Bible, He has used John Bunyan, sitting for 12 years in a miserable 17th century prison, to condense and articulate the biblical doctrine of prayer. If we never had any more instruction on prayer than the model Jesus gave us in Matt. 6:9-13 and Bunyan's definition, we might have much more to learn, certainly; but we would be reasonably educated on how to practice effective prayer.

We pray to God our Father; we pray sincerely and affectionately; we pray with the assistance of the Holy Spirit; we pray through Christ, who is our advocate at the right hand of God; we pray for the topics Christ gave us and the things God has promised and/or are according to His written Word; we pray with the goal of the good and advancement of His Church; we pray submitted to His will regarding the trials and circumstances of this present physical life; and we pray in faith.

Let's pray that Christ's Church will understand and endeavor to conform our prayer to what God has revealed in His Word; that we would profit greatly from the model prayer in Matt. 6:9-13 and the Biblical spectrum of prayer articulated for us by John Bunyan.

Father,

Help us to progress in our understanding of prayer. Help us to comprehend its structure and process as we read Scripture. Help us not to remain infants in our prayer, but to come into Your presence as mature children — to do serious eternal business with You. Help us take careful note of the prayers recorded in Scripture and learn from them.

Day 23

*Ask, and it will be given to you; seek and
you will find; knock, and the door will be
opened to you. For everyone who asks
receives; he who seeks finds; and to him
who knocks, the door will be opened.*
— *Matthew 7:7-8*

Like every other undertaking in human experience, attitude and determination have a great bearing on prayer. Lukewarm prayer affects God about the same way a lukewarm church affects Him (Rev. 2:14-16) — He is apparently as likely to spit one out as the other. There is a progression of intensity in Matt. 7:7-8: First we ask. We've brought the topic up with God concerning a specific need. We wait to see how He responds. We reassess if the Spirit of God is really motivating us to pray about it. We consider if it's in line with the will of God as Scripture reveals it. We check our motives — are we really asking this request so that God will be glorified?

Then something happens. Our sense of this need increases and accelerates — we begin to *seek* the Lord's involvement in this request because we see crisis on the horizon. So, we turn up the heat of our petition. "This," we tell ourselves, "really needs the attention of God! It's important to the coming Kingdom! It's a critical need in someone's life! There's no human help for this situation!" This petition is not just some mundane matter that mildly gains our passing interest — we must bring it to the Father. He is the only one who can sort this mess out.

Some time passes. We see little change in the situation. Things get no better. They may even tend to be getting worse. It is then that our desperation leads to an intensity that *knocks*. We MUST gain God's ear in the matter.

Like John Knox who said, "Give me Scotland or I die," we say, "I MUST have this request — regardless of the personal cost to me."

It's a probing question: What is the Holy Spirit motivating us to request of God that we are willing to pay any price personally to get?

> The strongest one in Christ's kingdom is he who is the best knocker. The secret of success in Christ's Kingdom is the ability to pray. The one who can wield the power of prayer is the strong one, the holy one in Christ's Kingdom. The most important lesson we can learn is how to pray.
>
> — E.M. Bounds
> *Purpose in Prayer*

Let's pray for all believers, that we would continue in prayer, listening to God the Holy Spirit as He increases our intensity until we are knocking at the LORD's door, because we MUST have what we ask.

Father,

Encourage us to pray with increasing intensity when we know that what we ask is a desire Your Spirit has motivated us about. May we not give up, or lose interest, or second-guess whether it is an appropriate petition or not. If You have repeatedly brought something to mind and the answer is truly for Your glory — may we ask — and seek — and knock.

Day 24

For no matter how many promises
God has made, they are "Yes" in Christ.
And so through him the "Amen" is
spoken by us to the glory of God.
— 2 Corinthians 1:20

It doesn't take long for children to learn an argument that usually prevails with parents when something doesn't work out for them as expected. "But you promised!" they wail. And there is Biblical support for this. Parents, as well as children, innately understand that the honor and character of any authority figure is undermined when they do not carry through on promises.

Charles Spurgeon was a Victorian gentleman whose way of speaking seems difficult to understand to the modern reader. But his content in the following quote is well worth sorting out. The original read:

Every promise of Scripture is a writing of God, which may be pleaded before Him with this reasonable request: "Do as Thou hast said." The Creator will not cheat His creature who depends upon His truth; and, far more, the Heavenly Father will not break His word to His own child. "Remember the word unto Thy servant, on which Thou has caused me to hope," is a most prevalent pleading. It is a double argument: It is Thy word, wilt Thou not keep it? Why hast Thou spoken of it if Thou wilt not make it good? Thou hast caused me to hope in it: wilt Thou disappoint the hope which Thou hast Thyself begotten in me?

Here is what Spurgeon is saying in modern English:

— Plead the promises You find in Scripture.
— The character of God prevents Him from breaking His word to His children. Remind God that You have found hope in what He has promised.
— Then plead this two-fold argument to God, "You've said it, LORD, so won't You keep it?"

Then a bold statement:

— "Why did You promise it if You didn't intend to keep it?"
— And last, but very boldly, "You are the One, LORD, who caused me to hope in it — so You surely won't leave me disappointed."

The promises of Scripture are a solid foundation for coming boldly to the Throne of Grace and the Bible is full of them. Would it not be a good prayer habit to mark the promises, find out who they are made to, be thankful for the ones already fulfilled, and argue the onwes appropriate to us, His Church, for what is yet to be fulfilled? They are solid gold "legal tender" to be used in prayer.

Father,

We would argue Your promise of 2 Cor. 1:20 itself: All Your promises are "yes" through Jesus Christ. Help us to recognize them, bring them to You, and agree with them — which is what we do when we say "Amen" to them. Help us learn that much of the heart of prayer is actually praying for what You have already promised to do. Help us to see those people and situations around us that are so desperately in need of what You have promised — and pray the promise for them boldly.

Day 25

Let us then approach the throne of grace with
confidence, so that we may receive mercy and
find grace to help us in our time of need.
— Hebrews 4:16

I was in labor with my first child for 17 hours, which is not really an unusual amount of time for a first pregnancy. Getting that baby from where it was to where it needed to be seemed like an absolute impossibility. I know the doctor — with his running in and out to check on things — meant well; but I wasn't convinced he could understand how I felt.

But then, my oldest sister walked in. She had taken time off work and had come to be with me. She had been through this same ordeal three times herself. She knew about the pain and the fear. "Your body knows what to do," she told me. "The baby will come, the pain will end, and you will forget all about this agony." I held her hand and believed what she told me, because she had been where I was.

Heb. 4:15, the verse preceding our text, says, "For we do not have a High Priest who is unable to sympathize with our weaknesses, but we have one who has been tempted in every way, just as we are — yet was without sin." We have a High Priest who has been where we are. Jesus knows all about what we are going through. He's experienced it all. He understands human suffering and human weakness. He has existed for all of eternity and knows His purposes will certainly come to pass. He knows what He's planned for us will be worth the short pain we go through in this life.

The book of Matthew ends with all power and all authority granted to Christ. He is the one in Daniel 7:14 who is prophetically given "authority, glory and sovereign power." Will not God give Him whatever He asks? It is because Christ is at this present moment at the right hand of God interceding for us that we can come before the Throne of Grace boldly and confidently and find understanding as well as mercy, grace, and help in time of need.

Let's pray for the world-wide Church, our own congregations, our pastors, our leaders, our teachers, and ourselves that we grasp the wonder of a sympathetic High Priest who knows us intimately and understands where we are in life, because our boldness in prayer is rooted in this truth.

Father,

We have a shared experience with Jesus. We have His under-standing about how painful this life can be. He knew temptation and disgrace, hunger and rejection, betrayal and abandonment. He's not going to be shocked by anything we bring to Him. He brings our prayer to You with a sympathetic regard for us and our problems, pleading His own blood as the reason You should hear us. As our High Priest, He makes it possible for us to approach Your throne confidently, finding mercy and grace for our needs.

Day 26

Then Jesus told his disciples a parable to show
them that they should always pray and not give up.
— Luke 18:1

We all learn from simple stories and illustrations. Who can forget the lessons of *Charlotte's Web* and how many times has it been used to teach children? Jesus, too, often used parables — simple, every-day stories — to teach His disciples.

Luke 18:1-8 is the parable Christ taught to teach us that we ought to continue praying and not quit. The parable is about a persistent woman who was trying to get a just judgment from an unjust judge. He would not hear her because her cause was just or because he had the responsibility to judge rightly — he heard her and gave her a just judgement because she never quit pestering him!

We are expected to make the comparison — if an unjust judge hears and gives justice because someone is persistent, then what will the righteous Judge of all the Earth do when His children call on Him persistently? He will not ignore them (v. 7).

Why does God want us to pray continually over a period of time? There are several reasons for this. Often, God wants to bring out maturity and Christlikeness in the one who prays. He also wants to work in the situation or person that is being prayed about. The LORD wants faith itself to be tested, strengthened, and purified — like silver in the crucible. And other times, like the child who gets things too early and too easily, if we receive things from the LORD without perseverance, there's more harm done than good. God, who works to bring things together for the good of His children (Rom. 8:28), knows far better than we exactly how and when His answers should be given. He may require persevering prayer because He is teaching us far more, and preparing us for far more, than what we are actually requesting.

It's interesting to note that Christ is the ultimate role model for persistent, persevering prayer. For over 2,000 years — right up to the present — Jesus has involved Himself in taking the prayers of His people to the Father's throne. He obeys the instruction of His Father in Psalm 2:

> *Yet have I set my king upon my holy hill of Zion. I will declare the decree: the LORD hath said unto me, Thou art my Son; this day have I begotten thee. Ask of me, and I will give thee the nations for thine inheritance, and the uttermost parts of the earth for thy possession.*
> *— Psalm 2:6-8 KJV*

From the time of God's eternal decree to place the nations under His authority and power, Jesus has been advocating for the complete fulfillment of Ps. 2:6-8 — with and through the prayers of His children who ask for His Kingdom to come and the will of God to be done. We are part of a great army of saints who give God no rest until these promises come to fulfillment.

Let's pray that:

- We might always pray and never quit.
- We might find great delight in reflecting Jesus who is our ultimate role model in patient, persevering prayer.

Father,

If Jesus intercedes persistently, then we should be no different. Help us to see through and beyond the intervening events of life that separate us from Your complete answers. If You have promised it — we know we have it. It's as good as done, no matter how long it takes.

But, O, Father — when we pray and must wait for the answer, please give us a faith as big as Mount Rushmore. Then teach us the holy art of mixing persevering prayer, Your promises, and a great faith so that prayer that once seemed the most agonizing and heavy to lift takes on a wondrous buoyancy and ascends effortlessly to Your throne.

Thank You, Father. Amen.

Day 27

*And will not God bring about justice for his
chosen ones, who cry out to him day and night?
Will he keep putting them off? I tell you, he will see
that they get justice, and quickly. However, when
the Son of Man comes, will he find faith on the earth?"*
— Luke 18:7-8

In addition to Christ showing us we should always pray and not give up, the parable of the persistent widow in Luke 18:1-8 makes a second point: In contrast to the unjust judge, what will the righteous Judge of all the Earth do when He is continually asked for justice? He will give it to His chosen ones quickly! It is obvious from this parable that our responsibility is to be continually crying out to God for justice — for the sake of His children.

We are to pray for justice to be enacted in our courts, in our laws, and in our institutions and authorities. We should pray for it to be maintained at every level of our society — our government, our law enforcement, our schools, our businesses, our media, and our homes. We need to pray for those who are forced to live under unjust governments, especially regarding the persecuted church. We should certainly pray for justice for those who have been martyred because they refused to deny the Lord (Rev. 6:9-11) and God of a certainty is going to give it.

Believers, we are in many ways like watchmen on the walls of our culture. There is great danger to any generation that does not value justice. Evil takes over when it is not upheld. Therefore, our duty to continually beseech God for justice is very great.

The parable in Luke 18:1-8 ends with an ominous question: "However, when the Son of Man comes, will he find faith on the earth (v. 8)?" Jesus doesn't assure us of the answer to this question. He leaves it open-ended and up to us to answer. I suspect the answer will be greatly affected by whether or not believers have persistently prayed and have not given up — right up to the hour that Christ comes.

God forbid that we fail to be people of faith and prayer. May we earnestly come before His throne and pray for the justice God has promised and will ultimately give.

Let's pray for the world-wide Church that:

- When Jesus comes, He will find us watching in faith and continuing in prayer.
- We bring all specific injustice we encounter to the Lord and ask that He intervene.

Father,

*Justice seems to be a more and more scarce commodity in our world, especially in areas where to believe in Jesus is an invitation to persecution. But the Westminster Shorter Catechism says You are "a Spirit, infinite, eternal, and unchangeable in [Your] being, wisdom, power, holiness, **justice**, goodness and truth" (emphasis the author's]. We trust You to enact ultimate justice for all the injustices that have been carried out on this earth.*

Day 28

Remember those in prison as if you were
their fellow prisoners, and those who are
mistreated as if you yourselves are suffering.
— Hebrews 13:3

I remember an incident in a mall one Christmas season. Shoppers were hurrying about on the upper level with their packages under their arms. Suddenly, everyone hurried to the rail and looked down at the floor below where a loud commotion drowned out the Christmas carols. There were cries, shouts, and what sounded like a small dog barking. Along with everyone else, I looked down and saw a group of special-needs children in wheelchairs and walkers being led through the mall on a shopping trip for the holidays. I couldn't help noticing the reaction of the shoppers around them. They were distancing themselves and keeping their eyes averted, not wanting to be involved. But then, I saw something wonderful. A young nurse with her hair in a ponytail went over to the child who seemed to be in the most distress. She put her arms around him, adjusted whatever was causing his outcry, and comforted him. Then she walked on, still with her arm on the child's shoulder, and smiled at the crowd as if to say, "It's okay. He's with me."

As of this writing, there are 195 countries in the world. Fifty of them severely persecute their people just because they follow Jesus. We may not be able to put our physical arms around the persecuted, suffering church. But we can do something better. We can bring them before God and pray as Heb. 13:3 instructs. When we do this, we reach across the miles and obstacles and affect what happens with these people because we are praying according to the will of God regarding them. None of them are outside the reach of our prayer. As we bring them before the LORD, we are identifying with them. Spiritually, we're putting our arms around them, saying, "It's okay. You're with me and Almighty God is with both of us."

There are organizations that communicate with the oppressed church and offer them practical help. Open Doors, Global Christian Relief, and The Voice of the Martyrs are three who maintain websites and ways to get involved. They can give us the names and situations of various individuals we can pray for and ways to extend practical help. If we are going to pray as God shows us, we're going to have to "Remember those in prison as if [we] were fellow prisoners, and those who are mistreated as if [we ourselves] are suffering" (Heb. 13:3).

Father,

You tell us in Your Word to carry each other's burdens. That instruction carries beyond just our own little corner of the world. We need to be just as interested and concerned and praying for someone in Northern Africa — who must walk miles to get drinkable water—as we are about our own broken faucet; or as concerned about the difficulty of believers in communist nations — who must avoid surveillance when they meet to worship — as we are about the repairs needed on our church parking lot.

Help us not to fall into the lazy habit of just praying in generalities. How can we know when You've answered us — and praise You for the answer — if we aren't specific? Father, I think we try Your patience when we don't tell You who we're praying for and what we want for them.

Day 29

I urge, then, first of all, that requests,
prayers, intercession and
thanksgiving be made for all people.
— 1 Timothy 2:1

When the Holy Spirit brings someone to mind — maybe someone we haven't seen for years, or someone we just saw in passing — it is a divine appointment to pray for them. It's very sobering to realize that there are people in this world that maybe *the only one on the face of the earth bringing them to the Throne of Grace, pleading God's intervention in their tremendous need,* is US.

When we tell someone we will be praying for them, it means we want to do something of eternal value for them. It's not a sign that we're totally stumped, that we don't have a clue what can be done in their seemingly hopeless situation. We need to overcome the thinking that prayer is a last resort, sort of a well-intended, but hopelessly ineffective act. Prayer is absolutely the most powerful and effective way we could possibly help them because we are calling on the all-powerful, all-knowing God of the Universe to get involved.

Prayer that's brought to the Mercy Seat in unity with Jesus, motivated and energized by the Holy Spirit, is the very best thing we can possibly do for hurting people. It reaches far beyond the actual situation they are in.

It affects spiritual realms and actions. It activates God's involvement to bring about their eternal good and His eternal glory. Their present plight is not the only thing we are praying for — we are praying to see God's hand be active in them for the rest of their lives.

Let's learn to wait on God as we pray. We are so programmed to want immediate gratification. We so often want to see lives changed or trials ended with the speed of pressing a button on the television remote that we often walk away from the situation without waiting for the LORD to act. We need to understand *God seldom zaps. He works on several fronts to bring things together.* When we sense the urge to pray for those the Holy Spirit brings to mind, it is an indication He is getting ready to work in their lives — and our prayer, wonderfully, is part of the process.

Let's pray that:

- We realize God could work in the lives of others by Himself without our help — but He chooses to use our prayer.
- We never offer to pray for someone apologetically — but trustingly and reassuringly.
- We realize God works in and through trials and difficulties toward good ends. God's purposes for us require time and patient faith.

Father,

It is an exciting thing to realize the Holy Spirit brings people to mind and motivates us to pray for them. Help us to be sensitive to it.

How awesome that You bring others to our thinking for a reason. Help us to take this opportunity very seriously because it's an indication You are getting ready to work in their lives through our prayer.

Day 30

But you, dear friends, build yourselves
up in your most holy faith
and pray in the Holy Spirit.
— Jude 1:20

And pray in the Spirit on all occasions
with all kinds of prayers and requests.
With this in mind, be alert and
always keep on praying for all the saints.
— Ephesians 6:18

I wish I could go back about 25 years in my life and learn what Scripture means when it says to pray while in the Spirit. I always thought it was just too difficult and complicated for anyone except very mature believers to comprehend, so I just skimmed over passages like Jude 1:20 and Eph. 6:18. What do these verses mean?

It might take a large volume to explore that question fully, but we should stress at the very beginning: *One does not have to be an old, experienced believer — one that knows the Scriptures like he knows his way to his own mailbox — in order to pray in the Spirit.* But we do have to have one principle in place: **We can't separate reading the Word of God and the work of the Holy Spirit in our hearts as we read.** In order to pray in the Spirit, both disciplines must be operating. Praying in the Spirit is not a product of the un-regenerate person spoken of in Eph. 4:20-22: It is produced from the regenerated (born again) heart of a believer referred to in verses 23-24 as they pray with the assistance of the indwelling Spirit of God. At the very least, to pray in the Spirit is to pray in connection to, and in agreement with the Holy Spirit — in cooperation with Him, dependent on Him, and willing to follow His leading as we read the Word.

Maybe it would help us understand how to pray in the Spirit if we not be in a hurry when we go to God in secret prayer; that we slow down and really enjoy a time of praise and worship and thanksgiving in His presence as we ponder the Scriptures. We might take some time just sitting in silence before God — waiting to sense in our spirit the still, small voice of the Holy Spirit.

Dr. Martyn Lloyd Jones says:

> You are aware of communion, a sharing, a give and take, if I may use such an expression. You are not dragging Yourself along; You are not forcing the situation; You are not trying to make conversation with somebody whom You do not know. No, no! The Spirit of adoption in You brings You right into the presence of God, and it is a living act of fellowship and communion, vibrant with life.
>
> *— Living Water*

How do we sense such a state of connection in prayer? It probably differs a little with each believer — but, as a general rule, I believe there are some common denominators we usually experience as we approach our Father to pray in the Spirit:

- As we read the Word and respond rightly to what God is telling us ...
- And as we become far more interested in what He is saying to us

than in what we so impatiently want to say to Him ...

- And as praise, worship, and thanksgiving give way to such wonder and awe that we are left breathless at WHO He is ...
- And we are left only able to shake our heads, because words fail ...
- It's then that the Holy Spirit of God within us brings to mind what we need for ourselves and others ...
- And we sense the Father asking us what we want.

It is crucial for believers to train themselves to pray with the Scriptures open in front of them, adjusting their prayer to what the Holy Spirit has inspired in the Word. But let's not just leave it at that; that is, with the mind engaged — but not the heart! Let's reach toward our Father from our inmost soul and spirit.

The reading of the Word and the leading of the Spirit are inextricably linked in praying in the Spirit. And so should they be linked with the heart throb of the worshiping believer.

Day 31

There were lots of challenges in writing this book — especially for someone who understands how a computer works about as well as they understand diesel engine repair. As I took each of the entries and placed them in this final manuscript, red lines and funny markings appeared in the margins. When I attempted to print out the entries, they came out of the printer occupying only a portion of the page. No matter what I did, I couldn't correct the problems. So, I got on the internet, described the situation, and got a whole list of sites that could help me. I chose one. What a catastrophe! I couldn't find the places they told me to go, my screen didn't look like their screen, I didn't have a clue what they were saying.

I asked the LORD for help, and He brought to mind my friend Jo Anne. I called her and she listened to my woes and asked a few questions. Then she gave me a series of very simple instructions and walked me through them. With each click, the problems cleared up and I was able to make my computer work and print the way I wanted.

In the same way, these verses in 1 Thessalonians 5:16-20 *are clear, simple, concise directions to help us practice praying in the Spirit.*

Rejoice evermore. Because joy is a component of the Spirit's fruit, we don't want to be doing anything contrary to His ministry in our attitude. Always choose joy in what God has done. Refuse griping.

Pray without ceasing. Put the habit of prayer in place in Your life — disciplined, consistent, honest, hungered after — always ready to go at the Spirit's prompting.

In everything give thanks; for this is the will of God in Christ Jesus concerning You. No matter what circumstances You find Yourself in, express thanks to God while You are undergoing them.

Quench not the Spirit. When the Holy Spirit urges us to follow what the Scripture is saying, don't throw a wet blanket over what He says and walk away. Have a sensitive ear toward Him and obey Him.

Despise not prophesyings. Don't get angry and rebel at the reading or preaching of the Word — listen with a submissive spirit. Respond to the Word and do what it instructs You to do.

But please remember — 1 Thess. 5:16-20 is NOT a procedure we go through like a checklist, and if we do, God guarantees this mechanical process will produce praying in the Spirit. But following the instruction in these five verses DOES produce a climate where the Spirit of God can work.

Father,

We realize that praying in the Spirit is not a one-time accomplishment. Rather, it's a day-by-day, one prayer-to-the next-prayer, endeavor. It's a response to both the Word and the Holy Spirit's leading at the same time. Help us to understand this truth.

The Word without the Holy Spirit's ministry, illumination, and conviction is like having knowledge without zeal; and trying to pray in the Spirit without the Word is like having zeal without knowledge. But both disciplines require the heart-climate of 1 Thess. 5:16-20. We need all three at the same time.

O LORD, our Lord,
How majestic is Your name in all the earth!
— Psalm 8:1

Day 32

*Finally, brothers, pray for us that the message
of the Lord may spread rapidly and be honored,
just as it was with you. And pray that we may
be delivered from wicked and evil
men, for not everyone has faith.*
— 2 Thessalonians 3:1-2

Remember when we were children in Sunday School and our version of a computer presentation was the old flannel graphs? I vaguely remember one where two armies were fighting in the background — swords drawn and chariots rumbling (Ex. 17:8-16). In the foreground, Moses is standing with his arms stretched toward heaven beseeching God for Israel to win. Two men stand at his side — Aaron and Hur. Then the story changes, and the teacher must make some fast adjustments to the picture. Moses is too tired to hold his arms up, she tells the kids; but when he puts them down, Israel starts to lose! When he can muster enough strength to lift them up again, Israel starts to win again! A good teacher would keep this going for a while, switching the picture. Arms up, "WINNING!!" the kids scream. Arms down — "LOSING!!" they scream again.

Then the inevitable happens. Moses gets so tired he can't lift his arms one more time. "So, do you know what Aaron and Hur do?" the teacher asks. "They stand on each side and *hold his arms up for him,*" she announces, and quickly changes the picture to show God responding and Joshua defeating the powerful Amalekite army.

What a picture of prayer! What a picture of our responsibility to pray daily for our pastors. They need our support in prayer. And what a picture of the commitment needed from a congregation.

Those who pray the effective prayer of godly people are the "special forces" of the Church. They stand like Aaron and Hur — supporting those who fight on the front lines of the spiritual battles. They may be behind the scenes, unnoted, unrecognized, perhaps unappreciated. That's okay. In eternity, God will recognize and reward their commitment and faithfulness.

Let's pray for our pastors, that:

- They would faithfully teach, reprove, correct, and instruct in righteousness (2 Tim. 3:16) ... that they would not be swayed from this course and be protected from threatening evil forces. That the wonder of the gospel would speed forth from their ministry.
- God would call the readers of this book to involve themselves in the "special forces" army of saints who know they are in spiritual warfare and would seriously hold up their pastors in continual prayer for specific needs.

Father,

We confess our failure in this area of responsibility. This ought not to be. Forgive us and help us to refuse a critical attitude, or lovelessness, or prayerlessness toward those You've placed over us. They desperately need the prayers of their people. Father, may we refuse the pitiful, generalized petition of "Bless our pastors." May we, instead, offer up HEAVY INTERCESSION for them.

May we pray that:

- You would give them the wisdom of Solomon and the steadfastness of Jeremiah. (1 Kings 3:1-14; Lam. 3:22, 23)
- You would give them a heart like David's; the perseverance of Moses, and the fire of Elijah. (1 Sam. 13:14; Deut. 34:10-12; 1 Kings 18)
- You would work in them to want, and to do, Your good will. (Phil. 2:13)
- You would protect and deliver them from evil. (Eph. 6:10-20)
- They would be "wise as serpents, and harmless as doves." (Matt. 10:16 KJV)
- They would be completely filled with God's Spirit, abide in Christ, and give prayer first priority in their day. (Eph. 5:18; John 15:7; Mark 1:35)
- You would shepherd them and would nourish their soul as they spend time in Your Word. (Ps. 23; Matt. 4:4)
- You would give fruitfulness to their ministry and enormous blessing to their families. (Ps. 126:6; Ps. 128:3-6)
- They would be men who understand their times, like the sons of Issachar in 1 Chron. 12:32 and would speak publicly on issues that destroy our church, our marriages, our homes, and our children — call sin, sin: for we in the congregations cannot repent without the conviction of the Word and Your Holy Spirit.
- You would encourage them, comfort them, and lead them to make their personal relationship with You the most important

thing in their lives — that it would be sweet and satisfying and passionate; that they would thirst for You, and meeting You in the secret prayer chamber would empower and guard their ministry. We love them and they are entitled to our daily intercession for them.

Day 33

Praise be to the Lord, who has given rest
to his people Israel just as he promised.
Not one word has failed of all the good
promises he gave through his servant Moses.
— 1 Kings 8:56

I have always had an unusual ability to find four-leaf clovers. When I walked in the mornings, I seldom returned home without 3 or 4 of the cheerful little green leaflets in my hand (which says something about my walking speed). I would press them in a big heavy photographer's book we kept on the coffee table in the den. My children were amazed at this ability because they had never found any more than a few four-leaf clovers in their entire lives.

One day, my daughters were looking at the big book where the clovers were pressed and laughing. One of them said to the other, "Wow! I didn't know there were that many four-leaf clovers in the whole world! How can Mom find so many while she's walking?"

I happened to be passing through the room and overheard them. "I see them," I said, "because I'm always looking for them."

Just as the grasses are filled with four-leaf clovers, the Scriptures are full of promises — but maybe we don't see them because we're not looking for them.

First Kings 8:56 is a comment Solomon makes at the dedication of the temple he built in Jerusalem. He marvels that God has kept His promises. Even since the time of Moses, none of them have failed. New Testament believers can make the same comment — none of God's promises will fail. It's easy to quickly read through portions of Scripture and miss how many promises they contain. We should see red flags pop up every time we come across a promise — not flags marking danger, but flags marking opportunity — because God's promises are vitally connected to prayer and its fulfillment. We can either praise God for promises fulfilled or entreat Him to fulfil the ones to come. They are assets on deposit in the bank of Heaven, waiting for us to find and appropriate and to remind the LORD of what He has said.

Let's pray that:

- We develop an eye for promises in Scripture — and that we pray for the fulfillment of those yet to come. They are rich veins to be mined in prayer.
- We be totally confident that no promise of God ever will fall to the ground. All of them either have been, or will be, fulfilled. May they comfort and encourage us as we come across them.

Father,

Psalm 32:10 says, "Many are the woes of the wicked, but the Lord's unfailing love surrounds the man who trusts in him." Thank You that Your love surrounds us as we trust in You. What a reassuring thought.

Psalm 34:17 says, "The righteous cry out, and the Lord hears them; he delivers them from all their troubles." Father, You know the specific problems we are having. We bring them to You and know that You help us through them and ultimately deliver us from them.

Second Corinthians 4:17 says, "For our light and momentary troubles are achieving for us an eternal glory that far outweighs them all." Father, we realize that whatever we're going through is in our lives for a purpose. It is not wasted suffering. It is accomplishing for us a heavy weight of worth in the eternal world. Just knowing that truth makes life's journey easier. You know what You are doing in our lives. We praise and thank You for it all. And would You give us what You have promised?

Day 34

But you are a chosen people, a royal priesthood,
a holy nation, a people belonging to God,
that you may declare the praises of him who
called you out of darkness into his wonderful light.
— 1 Peter 2:9

I remember a corporate dinner where people were standing around making small talk before the meal. I happened to be speaking to a lady whose husband had just been hired as the agricultural expert for the animal feed division. "Yes," she laughingly told me. "Ken was born for this job. His mother always said he was born with fertilizer in his shoes."

Believers are born for particular positions and activities, too. Here is a description of a few of them. We are spiritually born, Peter says, to be a chosen people, a "royal priesthood," a "holy nation," and "people belonging to God" (1 Pet. 2:9).

In this entry, let's focus on just one of these positions — the believers' privilege of being a royal priest. Think about it. We actually take the affairs and people in our own sphere of influence directly to the Throne of Grace and pray about them with the sure knowledge that God hears, and He acts.

Wow! Through prayer we are intimately involved with asking for God's intervention into life all around us. If we pray in the Spirit, our prayer is vitally connected to the sovereign purposes of God — even in the little things and in the lives of those around us.

Yet, there is another wonder to being a royal priest:

> When the Lord divided Canaan among the tribes of Israel, Levi received no share of the land. God said to him simply, "I am thy part and thine inheritance," (Num. 18:20 KJV) and by those words made him richer than all his brethren, richer than all the kings and rajas who have ever lived in the world. And there is a spiritual principle here, a principle still valid for every priest of the Most High God.
>
> The man who has God for his treasure has all things in One. Many ordinary treasures may be denied him, or if he is allowed to have them, the enjoyment of them will be so tempered that they will never be necessary to his happiness. Or if he must see them go, one after one, he will scarcely feel a sense of loss, for having the Source of all things he has in One all satisfaction, all pleasure, all delight. Whatever he may lose he has actually lost nothing, for he now has it all in One, and he has it purely, legitimately and forever.

— A.W. Tozer
The Pursuit of God

Let's pray for the world-wide Church, our own congregations, our pastors, our leaders, our teachers, and ourselves that we take very seriously being royal priests. It allows us to stand and intercede between God and man, and its practice gives us great insight into God being our Great Treasure.

Father,

Just the phrase "royal priesthood" (1 Pet. 2:9) is astounding. We belong to a royal family, because we are Your children — the King of the Universe. And we now participate with You as go-be-tweens between You and the people we are praying for.

Help us to grasp the truth that our prayer is effective. There's no prison so secure, or government so restrictive, or circumstances so bad, that our prayer cannot penetrate. There are no people so resistant to Your truth that our prayer doesn't make an impact.

Our royal priesthood is a large part of our identity — we are born of You, our Father — to this honored position. Help us practice it with enthusiasm and wisdom!

Day 35

Remember the former things, those of long ago;
I am God, and there is no other;
I am God, and there is none like me.
I make known the end from the beginning,
from ancient times, what is still to come.
I say, My purpose will stand,
and I will do all that I please.
— Isaiah 46:9-10

Here's one of the questions believers always seem to struggle with as they attempt prayer: If God is sovereign — and we certainly know He is — then, how does prayer work? What if we are praying and it's not part of His sovereign will? And if His sovereignty trumps our petitions, then why should we pray? In my own case, I couldn't understand the emphasis the Bible had on prayer, and yet there seemed a contradictory truth that God always does what is according to His own will. I couldn't put these truths together.

There was a good article on this topic on the January 13, 2020, desiringGod.org website. It was written by Marshall Segal, one of the staff writers, and is entitled, "What Difference Will Prayer Make?" Here are some quotes from what he wrote:

"While we, as modern people, may feel some tension between the sovereignty of God and prayer, desperate, faithful, praying saints in Scripture do not seem to share our struggle — and God is not afraid to intimately knit his sovereignty and prayer together, especially in times of serious need."

"The sovereign God hangs the universe on the prayers of His people, and then inspires and empowers us to pray."

"God makes our humble, dependent, expectant cries for help the instruments of what he does in the world."

"The absolute sovereignty of God, over every detail of our lives, is the hope and foundation for our praying."

"When God makes and carries out his plans, he plans for us to pray."

[quoted by permission]

Father,

We tend to see the puzzle of resolving Your perfect will with our desires pictured as a graph with two parallel lines — where Your will is a horizontal line across the top and our desires are a horizontal line across the bottom — and so many times we can't see how the two lines can ever intersect.

That's why we love these quotes! This puzzle is resolved by the ministry of the Holy Spirit. Our prayer and Your sovereignty are not at odds — they are not two parallel lines going on into infinity without ever meeting — but are perfectly blended together through the work of Your Spirit. We can pray for anything the Holy Spirit lays heavy on our hearts, and then rest in how God orchestrates it — bringing it all together according to His will.

- In Scripture we see God commit Himself — and all His resources — to His children in His promises.
- In His eternal omniscience, God always makes His promises consistent with His will, His character, His attributes, His plans, His purposes, and His eternal decrees.
- Because of the work of the Holy Spirit in the hearts of His people, God's decrees — His promises — and the prayers of His redeemed people are divinely connected and eternally bound together.

So, we may safely say, "Our prayer and God's sovereignty are not at odds — they are not two parallel lines going off into infinity without ever meeting." They are perfectly and peaceably brought together in the sovereign, eternal plan of God and the purified desires and prayers of His people.

> Wondrous ocean, who can sound thee?
> Thine own eternity is round thee ...
> Majesty Divine!
> Majety Divine!
>
> — Frederick W. Faber 1920

Day 36

... but those who hope in the LORD will renew their strength. They will soar on wings like eagles; they will run and not grow weary; they will walk and not be faint.
— Isaiah 40:31

We live in a period of history that expects instant gratification. We're accustomed to fast food, immediate entertainment, and information from the internet at the touch of a button. We even demand instantaneous boiling water from our coffee makers. But God does not work that way. Often, prayers that are persistently prayed in the very darkest hours of our lives are answered in marvelous ways — far above all that we can "ask or imagine" (Eph. 3:20) — *but many years after their utterance.*

Prayers Joseph offered up agonizingly — for around 13 years — are finally answered, propelling him in less than a day from the prison cells of Egypt to the throne room of Pharaoh.

Daniel was taken as a young man — maybe 16? — in the Babylonian Captivity. He prayed three times a day with his face toward Jerusalem. But he endured through the reigns of several kings, including Nebuchadnezzar, Belshazzar and into the reign of Darius the Mede before God sends Gabriel with a history-encompassing answer.

Waiting is an inflexible discipline for fervent prayers that avail much.

Prayer follows the law of maturation — like seed to fruit-bearing. Prayer is an investment. It is, so many times, in need of other elements. It waits on God's purposes, His will, our requests, and our maturing application of faith — all to intersect in His timing. It takes patient waiting for God to work so that "all things work together for good" (Rom. 8:28)." The surprising thing is — prevailing prayer is so much, much bigger than the original petitioner's intent! It impacts a far greater number of people and events than the one praying had in mind. Prevailing prayer reaches into eternity!

There are times, however, when prayer is answered immediately. Isaiah had not gotten out of the king's courtyard when he was called back to take part in the answer to Hezekiah's prayer (2 Kings 20:1-11). Peter cried for help and was pulled out of the water immediately (Matt. 14:28-31). But these accounts are the exception rather than the rule. In the majority of cases, prayer must be offered perseveringly, with a willingness to wait on the LORD's time and the LORD's way. Adoniram Judson (1788-1850), missionary to Burma said:

> God loves importunate [persistent] prayer so much that
> He won't give us much blessing without it.

We learn two very valuable spiritual lessons when we pray persistently — our faith is matured and purified, and waiting on God is worth the wait!

Let's ask God to do what He must do in our lives to teach us the art of persistent, patient prayer. May we wait on God and experience our strength being renewed. Let's ask Him to give us the sense of being lifted on eagle's wings in renewed energy and passion for prayer.

Father,

Help us not be afraid of asking You to do in our lives what You need to do to make us persistent, patient intercessors. Help us view every trial and difficulty as Your means of making us like Christ, thus more able to pray. Help us to view this petition like teenagers view riding a roller-coaster: it's exciting, exhilarating, and totally safe.

Day 37

Response to Persistent Praying

Okay, Father,

We accept that you love persistent prayer, and we understand most of the reasons for it. Praying over a protracted period of time is illustrated in the prayers of such saints as Joseph, Daniel, Isaiah, and Anna — so we shouldn't be surprised that it's a discipline we need to practice, too.

We realize there are great lessons to be learned from waiting. Things like patiently persevering despite obstacles; being willing to examine our lives and our motives; a practical understanding of just how far-reaching your answer to prayer can be. Waiting can affect many different people in many different ways. It has even changed the course of events! While waiting, we can rest in your wisdom. Your answers don't create more problems down the road than they solve in the immediate. They are perfect answers.

We are also willing to wait because, so many times in Scripture, we see answers that are far greater than the original prayer. Abraham had no conception of what would happen in answer to his prayer for a son. Paul prayed for the gospel to spread but had no inkling of the millions and millions of believers that would be the result.

We're thankful, Father, and greatly encouraged that in all the information about prayer we can find in the pages of the Bible, there are very few times when You tell people to stop praying. You told Moses to stop asking when he wanted to be allowed to enter the Promised Land. You told him not to ask again, that Your mind was made up. When Jerusalem was facing the exile to Babylon, You told Jeremiah not to pray for the people anymore — the time of Your judgment had come, and Jerusalem was going to fall to Nebuchadnezzar. Then we can look at Paul. When he asked for his physical disability to be removed, You simply told him Your grace was sufficient in the circumstance. He didn't ask again.

There are maybe a couple of other instances in Scripture where You tell someone not to pray for specific things, but very few. We can be encouraged that if our requests are not contrary to Scripture, and we continue to sense the Holy Spirit urging us to pray about a particular request, we can keep persistently asking.

We love You, Father, and thank You for the wondrous privilege of prayer.

Day 38

*The end of all things is near. Therefore, be clear
minded and self-controlled so that you can pray.*
— 1 Peter 4:7

Because I'm extremely interested in prayer, I talk to a lot of people about it. It's surprising how many times they've told me their prayer habits are closely linked to the physical habits in their lives. What time they make themselves get up in the morning; being in the habit of a specific time and place for reading the Word; refraining from certain activities because they feel it hampers their prayer life — all these are issues of self-control for the sake of their prayers.

At the very least, self-control is a tremendous asset in prayer. *Strictly speaking, it is a necessity.* Why? Because it is a fruit of the Spirit. Self-control says "no" to the whims of the flesh, and "yes" to the leading of the Spirit and the Scripture He inspired. If we are not led by the Spirit in what we think, what we say, what we do, and what we pursue — it's not likely we are submitting to being led in prayer by Him either.

Self-control is exercised when we look beyond the impulses and appetites of the moment to grasp bigger, and better, and more vitally important opportunities in the future. We might need to cut out caffeine after 3:00 pm, for instance, because it interferes with our sleep and thus affects getting up early for prayer. Or maybe we find ourselves needing to curtail the kinds of books we read, or the programs we watch on television, or the movies we attend — because they dishonor God and negatively affect the quality of our prayer life. We learn we need to refrain from anything that puts something between us and the Father in prayer.

Restraining ourselves from even legitimate things helps us practice self-control, thus strengthening our prayer life. Fasting does not always have to be about food. We can come apart for a time from innocent enjoyments — like reading, or sleeping later, or hobbies, or chocolate! — and use our hunger for them to remind us of some great need we should bring to God. Just the physical sensation of missing a legitimate pleasure can sharpen our focus and intensity in prayer.

"Time is short," Peter tells us. "The end of all things is at hand..." Therefore, it's necessary that we be "self-controlled and sober-minded (1 Peter 4:7)" so that we can effectively pray.

Let's pray that we will learn to practice self-control
for the sake of our prayers.

Father,

We are living in a time when self-indulgence is the norm and self-denial is almost non-existent. Since we are all somewhat the products of our current culture, we really need Your help in grasping the importance of self-control to our prayer life.

But Your Word is timeless — we are not exempt from the discipline of self-control even if it isn't a popular discipline in our day. It is greatly important; it lessens the hold of this world on our souls. The lack of control over our own spirit leaves us vulnerable to spiritual attack. Help us to practice it, we pray.

Day 39

But the tax collector stood at a distance.
He would not even look up to heaven,
but beat his breast and said, "God,
have mercy on me, a sinner ..."
— *Luke 18:13*

As my husband and I were raising our daughters, there were several household rules covering things like chores and character, schoolwork and curfews, and any number of incidental issues critical to rearing children. Most of these rules were reinforced through the years with minimal repercussions when they were broken. Occasionally, there were dire threats of consequences if behavior in certain areas didn't change, but usually verbal reminders worked if we carried through with consequences when offenses were repeated. But there was one rule that carried immediate discipline. There were no patient grace periods and no threats when this happened. We acted immediately. It was their posture — not physically — but the posture of attitude. We did not ignore disrespect because it destroys the ability of parents to instill wisdom and good character and a healthy God-view in their children.

Likewise, the *posture of humility* is one of the governing principles in prayer because pride destroys our ability to listen to God when He works in our lives. Humility sets the tone for the right relationship between the praying believer and the LORD, and the prayers of the Pharisee and the tax collector in Luke 18:9-14 illustrate it well. Where the tax collector admits he is a sinner and is ashamed to even approach God, his prayer that God would be merciful to him is answered. He goes away right with God. But the Pharisee tells God he doesn't rob, doesn't commit evil or adultery, fasts every week and gives tithes. The Pharisee believes he is already righteous and deserves God's ear. It doesn't occur to him that his pride is a deal-breaker. His prayer is not answered: he goes away unjustified.

The truth is, prayer that is proud, demanding, self-confident, self-focused and unheeding to God's Word doesn't go any higher than the ceiling. We can't manipulate or deceive the LORD about our motives. He can read our thoughts before we speak them (Ps. 139:4).

There's room for honest emotion in prayer — yes. Self-serving temper tantrums — no.

Humble and contrite hearts — yes. Proud, self-righteous spirits — no.

God has a loving, compassionate attitude toward His children when we come to Him with our needs and petitions and cares. He listens and sympathizes very well. He wants to say "yes" when it is for our good and His glory. But He does not tolerate a posture of pride.

Let's pray that:

- We come before God in prayer with totally honest hearts and humble attitudes.
- We realize we are not only children coming to a wise Father, but we are also in many respects, beggars coming to the Great King; and we would adjust our attitude accordingly.

Father,

We are strange creatures: We admire humility in others and despise their pride, but stubbornly hang on to pride in our own hearts and find it very difficult to humble ourselves. Help us to be people who can easily say to others, "I was wrong — will You forgive me?" And help us become like little children in our attitude as we come to You in prayer.

Day 40

Devote Yourselves to prayer,
being watchful and thankful.
— Colossians 4:2

When we search the Scriptures for the LORD to show us how to pray, it's often surprising how simple some of the lessons are. It doesn't take a rocket scientist to figure out what He's showing us in Col. 4:2. A small child, if we explain the meaning of the words, can follow these instructions: Be *devoted* to prayer. Have an attitude of *watchfulness* when You pray. Exhibit *thankfulness* when You pray.

This instruction, like so many other teachings regarding prayer, stresses attitudes of the heart. What do we really value in our inner person? What catches our sympathy and our time commitment? Are we thankful to God for the indescribable treasure He has made available to us in Christ? All three of these questions are components in some of the first lessons the LORD teaches us about prayer.

Are we devoted to prayer? That is, are we loyally connected to it? Are we committed to prayer enough to make room for it in our lives — even willing to eliminate other time-consuming pursuits to give it priority? Do we believe God hears and answers prayer to the point that we persistently practice it? When we come right down to the bottom line of Christianity, prayer is one of the greatest evidences that we have faith in God.

Exhibiting watchfulness in prayer is not so hard to understand. It calls for us to be alert to what's going on around us, because there's a need for prayer everywhere we look. Praying people should be like night nurses — alert to the buzzers of their patients; like sentries in times of war — watching for the enemy; like mothers — sensitive to the needs of little ones.

Expressing thankfulness in prayer reflects a character trait wise parents teach their children from the time they can talk, because it is a root that produces so many other good traits. Gratitude and humility grow out of thankfulness. Appreciation for others is built into our souls when we are thankful. We acknowledge that, for us to receive free gratis, someone else must sacrifice. The poisonous attitude of entitlement, and its ugly offspring, petulance — abhorrent to God — is erased. God cares about these underlying character issues when we come to Him in prayer. An attitude that's flippant, proud, ungrateful, demanding, or selfishly entitled won't get far. We all have problems with those attitudes occasionally. The antidote? Thankfulness.

Let's pray for the world-wide Church, for our own congregations, for our pastors, our leaders, our teachers, and ourselves that:

- We be devoted to prayer.
- We be watchful in prayer.
- We be thankful in prayer.

Father,

These three elementary instructions — a devotion to prayer, exhibiting watchfulness in prayer, and expressing thankfulness in prayer — are not hard to comprehend; but they demand a self-discipline we often find hard to practice. Would You, through Your Holy Spirit, remind us of these admonitions when we get lax and let them fall by the wayside? Would You remind us that interaction with You is worth the effort of practicing these virtues? They may be simple, but they are powerful.

Day 41

Remember those in prison as if
you were their fellow prisoners,
and those who are mistreated
as if you yourselves were suffering.
— Hebrews 13:3

Sometimes God gives us specific topics to pray about. Hebrews 13:3 is one of them. The LORD would have us remember that there's no such thing as the free church and the suffering church. We are one body — and if one of our members is suffering, we are all suffering.

Christian persecution is extremely prevalent world-wide. Even by conservative estimates, the number of Christians killed every year is in the thousands. At least 50 countries persecute Christians within their borders. Terrorist attacks, church burnings, the destruction of property, unjust treatment and human trafficking are not uncommon. Christian population is plunging drastically in the Middle East.

Open Doors, a group ministering to the persecuted, estimates there are 70,000 Christians in North Korea held in concentration camps. They also reveal this astounding fact: 245 million Christians suffer high levels of persecution all over the world.

The Voice of the Martyrs, an organization started by Richard Wurmbrand, *Tortured for Christ*, says, "The primary request of persecuted

Christians around the world is not for money or protection from those who persecute them. Instead, they first ask for prayer. The Voice of the Martyrs urges Christians to pray that the persecuted will:

1. Sense God's presence.
2. See God open doors for them to witness for Him.
3. Be able to forgive and love their persecutors.
4. Experience the joy of the Lord, even amid suffering.
5. Know You and other Christians are praying for them."

— Persecution.com 1/3/19
[quoted by permission]

In an open email of January 30, 2020, Open Doors wrote: "Today by the time You go to sleep, eight Christians will have died for their faith." That's a staggering statistic.

"... research for Open Door's 2020 World Watch List reveals that each day, eight people were martyred for their faith in the top 50 countries ranked on the list.With 260+ million Christians facing high levels of persecution for their faith, persecution against Christians is at its highest in modern history."

— opendoorsusa.org
[quoted by permission]

Please pray for the persecuted Church that:

- Through the fruit and the ministries of the Holy Spirit in their inner man, they would miraculously sense God's presence.
- God would open doors for them to witness for Him.
- They, by God's enablement, can forgive their persecutors.
- Joy would abound and flow over their souls — and that the joy of the Lord will be their source of unexplainable, unending strength.
- They would sense God's people faithfully praying for them.
- These requests from persecuted believers would focus our prayers on the really important issues...that we have the mindset of the church at Smyrna in Rev. 2:8-11.

Ah, Father,

We mourn the suffering the persecuted Church must endure. Will You give Your angels charge over them, deliver them from the evil one, and remind us daily of their desperate need for our prayer support? Will You assure them their brothers and sisters have not forgotten them?

Day 42

*"It is written," he said to them, 'My house
will be called a house of prayer,' but You
are making it a 'den of robbers.'"*
— Matthew 21:13

Wouldn't it be a great and wonderful and powerful thing if the Church today was known, first and foremost, across the entire world, as Matt. 21:13 indicates: A House of Prayer?

In Isaiah 56:7, partially quoted by Jesus as He is driving the money-changers out of the temple in Matt. 21:13, it says:

> "... these [outcasts from Israel] I will bring to my holy mountain, and make them joyful in my house of prayer; their burnt offerings and their sacrifices will be accepted on my altar; for my house shall be called a house of prayer for all peoples."

E.M. Bounds, a prolific writer on prayer, was a man who mourned the prayerlessness of the church in his day. He was a man who had far more in common with the fiery Elijah than most men — a person who never backed down. He hits us between the eyes with truth about the Church's lack of prayer and the pathetic state that such neglect produces. He writes:

"Many persons believe in the efficacy of prayer, but not many pray. Prayer is the easiest and the hardest of all things; the simplest and the sublimest; the weakest and the most powerful; its results lie outside the range of human possibilities — they are limited only by the omnipotence of God.

"... The Church seems almost wholly unaware of the power God puts into her hand; this spiritual carte blanche on the infinite resources of God's wisdom and power is rarely, if ever used — never used to the full measure of honoring God ... .

"Our people are not a praying people."

— *Purpose in Prayer* excerpts
E.M. Bounds

Pity the local church that has buildings and money and talent and programs, but neglects prayer. Pity the country that has no intercessors — where they are as scarce as hen's teeth. Pity the pastor whose people neglect intercession on his behalf, leaving him frazzled and harried and discouraged — ripe for burn-out.

Believers, *we are* the "house of God" (1 Peter 2:5). We must be about teaching prayer's principles, practicing them, and taking God at His word. God will most certainly do what He must do in His Church to make sure His house will ultimately "be called a house of prayer for all peoples" (Is. 56:7). But wouldn't we rather learn to be praying people in pleasant times and easy situations, rather than needing to be brought to hard, hard circumstances — like our persecuted brothers and sisters — in order to learn the lesson?

Let's pray for believers that:

- We would value prayer — first and foremost — as the boiler room — the power source — for all of life and ministry. We would seek to learn it, teach it, and practice it well.
- We would realize we *are* God's house, and we *must* be a house of prayer.

Father,

E.M. Bound's quote seems to soak into our souls, and we can't forget it. In all honesty, we must admit we have been among those who believe in prayer but find it so hard to consistently practice. LORD, help us to see that there are times when prayer is hard; but it is the simplest and the most sublime; the weakest, and the most powerful. Amazingly, we are involved in standing back and seeing Your omnipotence when we pray. Would You give us a new generation of praying saints?

Day 43

He who did not spare his own Son,
but gave him up for us all — how
will he not also, along with him,
graciously give us all things?
— Romans 8:32

The LORD is not a God Who does things in half-measures or slipshod procedures. He decreed an *epic, human-history-encompassing* plan, and He advances it forward in an orderly, methodical, certain fashion. Nowhere do we see it carried forward any more clearly than in the promises of Romans 8:28-39: All things will work together for our good; no one can ultimately be against us; God will give us all things; Christ intercedes for us; nothing can separate us from God's love in Christ; we are more than conquerors. He is going to "along with him [Christ], graciously give us all things" (Rom. 8:32).

Of course, these promises are given to a certain group of people — to those who trust Him. In eternity past, these believers were foreknown by God and predestined to be like Jesus Christ. He "called" these people, "justified" them, and "glorified" them (Rom. 8:30). It's interesting that all these verbs are in the past tense. It's as good as already done.

Called, justified, and glorified — these are enormous concepts! They are huge spiritual transactions that move forward the purposes of

God for His redeemed. Each one of them must be accomplished for the intended end to be a reality.

> *And I heard a loud voice from the throne saying, "Now the dwelling of God is with men, and he will live with them. They will be his people, and God himself will be with them and be their God."*
> — Rev. 21:3

We can start in Genesis 1 and follow this epic plan through the entire Bible. God created a world; made people male and female in His own image; then after sin entered, He promised a redeemer. He called out Abraham and promised him descendants as numerous as the stars in the sky, a promised land, and a heritage that blesses the nations. After Israel was in slavery in Egypt four hundred years, the LORD raised up Moses, led Israel out of Egypt, gave the law, established the idea of sacrifice for sin, and delivered to them the promised land. He established the Davidic kingdom; endured with Israel through the years of the kings; and sent prophets who communicated His will and foretold both judgement and glory for the nation.

Then God sends Jesus, the promised Messiah. He was crucified, but the resurrection takes place; the salvation message goes out; the Church is established; believers become new creations in Christ; the Holy Spirit comes to indwell and sanctify those who trust Christ; and God begins a work in them that will continue to the day of Christ's return. He transforms believers by renewing their minds. Through it all, He has bidden his believers to pray.

Called, justified, and glorified — we can follow God's hand steadily working through history to bring many believers to share His Kingdom and His glory.

If God has done all this — will He not give us all things? Will He allow anything to thwart His purposes for His people? *Will He not answer our prayer as we pray according to His Word?*

Let's pray for the world-wide Church, our own congregations, our pastor(s), our leaders, our teachers, and ourselves that:

- Our faith be enlarged until we can grasp that God gives us all things — including the privilege of answered prayer.
- We comprehend that our prayer being answered is bound up and included in the certainty of God hearing and answering Christ, our Intercessor.

Day 44

So Jacob was left alone, and a man wrestled with him til daybreak. When the man saw that he could not overpower him, he touched the socket of Jacob's hip so that his hip was wrenched as he wrestled with the man. Then the man said, "Let me go, for it is daybreak."

But Jacob replied, "I will not let you go unless you bless me."

The man asked him, "What is your name?"

"Jacob," he answered.

Then the man said, "Your name will no longer be Jacob, but Israel, because you have struggled with God and with men and have overcome."

— Genesis 32:24-28

If the verses in this text leave you scratching your head, don't be surprised. Believers have always pondered and puzzled over this portion of

Scripture. Verse 32 of this passage indicates this was no ordinary angel Jacob wrestled — but the pre-incarnate Jesus Christ! It begs the question, why was this wrestling necessary? Couldn't the Lord have won effortlessly by paralyzing Jacob or striking him to the ground? Does God resist us in prayer? Is He reluctant to give what He has already promised? Jacob was on his way back to his father's house. He was returning at the LORD's direction and with His promise for protection. But he learns his brother, Esau, is meeting him with an army of 400 men! The proverbial chickens seem to be coming home to roost, because some 20 years before, Jacob had stolen Esau's birthright through lies and deception. Esau had vowed to kill him over it, and now Jacob is afraid and very much in need of God's protective blessing.

So, what does wrestling have to do with it? Why does Jacob refuse to let go until he receives God's blessing? What does the LORD want His Church to take from this narrative?

Often, for God to purify our desires, to make us face the truth of our own sinfulness, develop our passion and persistence and determination — to focus us on the really important things, the eternal things — He brings us to the point of critical faith choices. He brings us to the place of life-changing priorities and direction, a change in our prayer life that causes us to press through our own fear of personal cost. Jacob had gotten Esau's rightful blessing by deception — but he will not get God's blessing that way. He's going to have to recognize the truth about himself and persist — *because he must have God's blessing.*

Like Jacob, we sometimes find ourselves wrestling with whether we back off from what we know will exact a personal cost. The LORD wrestles with us over these issues because He wants us to be satisfied with nothing less.

For instance:

> What if we are praying for the salvation of a person we love, but fear what God may have to do to bring them to Himself? It scares us.

What if we're praying for our church — for conviction of sin and repentance — but fear the pain and sorrow and embarrassment this could bring to innocent people?

What if we're praying for our nation — but fear the hardship and judgment God may have to bring for our prayers to be answered?

It's very significant that the Angel pronounces to Jacob that in his wrestling he had prevailed with God and with man. *Having power with God in prayer, he will also have power to affect men — even for the rest of eternity.* Jacob's name was changed to Israel — "God contends" — and he was a marked man for the rest of his life. So should we want to be as well because God contends in the battles for those He marks.

Let's pray for the world-wide Church that we be willing to wrestle through our own doubt and personal fear in order to prevail with God and with men.

Day 45

*His master replied, "Well done, good
and faithful servant! You have been
faithful with a few things; I will put
you in charge of many things. Come
and share your master's happiness."*
— Matthew 25:21

The point of the parable of the talents in Matt. 25:14-30 is that believers are given resources to invest for the Kingdom. We can look forward to the day we hear the King of kings say these same words to us! Our abilities, spiritual gifts, resources, and opportunities can be invested in the Kingdom, and we will give an account for them. But the reward is huge when we do.

Prayer is not the only investment believers make, but there is no greater investment of time than time invested in prayer. Prayer is not the only work believers take part in, but there is no greater work than the work of prayer. Prayer is not the only stewardship believers are responsible for, but there is no more vital stewardship responsibility than prayer. The Scriptures are the mine where gold, silver and precious stones are hidden — but the Advocacy of Jesus, the intercession of the Holy Spirit, and the prayers of the saints are the excavator that extracts them. No genuine eternal work happens without prayer, because "For from him and through him and to him are all things. To him be the glory forever! Amen" (Rom. 11:36). All things that are done *through Him* would not be complete without Christ's intercessory work between the saints and the Father. And believers participate in this work when they pray.

The good news — the *really* good news — is that the weakest believer, the frailest saint, the most timid personality, can be like one of David's mighty men — able to do spiritual warfare valiantly. If they come before the Throne of Grace and offer up prayer in unity with Christ and the Holy Spirit, they are the best investors, the most productive workers, and the most faithful stewards, because, as Spurgeon has written, "Prayer is the "slender nerve that moves the muscle of omnipotence."

Let's pray for the world-wide Church, our own pastor(s), our leaders, our teachers, and ourselves that we learn to invest in prayer. That we realize its absolute necessity in all work and all stewardship.

Father,

We love the fact that no matter where we are in this world, what our physical condition is, what our living conditions are, what our financial resources are, how educated we are or how simple — we can, through prayer, take part in investing real and lasting assets in real and lasting ventures. Thank You for the future "world without end" (Eph. 3:21 KJV).

Day 46

Thus saith the Lord God; I will yet
for this be enquired of by the house
of Israel, to do it for them; I will
increase them with men like a flock.
— Ezekiel 36:37 KJV

E.M. Bounds lamented that the Church of his time was not a Church of prayer. He made that statement out of frustration because he was an unparalleled exhorter to prayer. He was a man who carried a bright lantern and had traveled so far down the road of intercession that he continually turned and beckoned frantically, amazed that the rest of us lagged so far behind. He can be forgiven if he, at times, wondered if we were back there at all.

But God has never left His people without their intercessors.

The Old Testament had Hannah, Daniel, Hezekiah, and Isaiah. It had Samuel, David, and Asaph. There was Moses, Job, Noah, Esther, Jeremiah, and Solomon.

The New Testament Church made prayer one of their four exclusive focused priorities (Acts 2:42), and they had Paul, whose prayers are felt even today.

Church history is sprinkled with saints like Polycarp, Augustine, Luther, Calvin, Zwingli, and Wycliffe. We've had Bunyan and Isaac Watts.

In later days we've had Mueller, Madame Guyon, Murray, Chadwick, and Brainard. Recent history has seen Corrie Ten Boom, Ruth Bell Graham, and, of course, E.M. Bounds.

The truth is, God has given the Church a mighty army of unknown, unacclaimed heroes and heroines who have quietly stood in God's presence and prayed down God's intervention on the course of this world. Mothers and fathers unnumbered are among that throng. Generals like Thomas (Stonewall) Jackson are there. Miners and shopkeepers and frontier settlers, and teachers, and corporate managers, and preachers, and children's Sunday School teachers — all these, and many more from all walks of life, God has strategically placed as His intercessors, because He has ordained prayer as the method by which we receive from Him all that He delights to give to His Son and to His Church.

May He continue — in our darkening
days — to call out intercessors.

Let's pray for ourselves and all believers, that we would respond to God's call and pray according to the Scriptures as serious present-day, prevailing intercessors.

Father,
May we be numbered with the saints who have called on Your name in spirit and in truth. May our prayer be offered up before Your throne and mixed with the prayers of all the saints referred to in Rev. 8:4. Please don't leave our day without intercessors who know how to pray led by Your Holy Spirit. Work in us to bring us to Your throne so that we can ask, and You will answer us with "awesome deeds of righteousness" (Psalm 65:5).

Day 47

My prayer is not for them alone.
I pray also for those who will
believe in me through their message,
that all of them may be one, Father,
just as you are in me and I am in
you. May they also be in us so
that the world may believe
that you have sent me.
— John 17:20-21

Why do we pray? What is the purpose of prayer?

Ask believers whose opinions you respect these questions, and you will likely get as many answers as the number of people you approach. Ask Charles Spurgeon and he would likely say, "The purpose of prayer is to gain the ear of God." Ask John Piper, and judging by the gist of his writings, he would probably tell you prayer is for spiritual warfare. Ask E.M. Bounds, who wrote nine books on the subject, and he would clobber you over the head with so many trumpeting answers you'd be frantically trying to write them all down two weeks after you asked.

A.W. Tozer, who so much emphasized the personal interaction with God, would probably say the purpose of prayer is to bring you into constant communion with God the Father, and Andrew Murray, who wrote *With Christ in the School of Prayer* would insist we pray to practice the most magnificent work people can be involved in. Brother Lawrence would tell You prayer's purpose is so we can be in God's presence, and Samuel Chadwick might remind You of his famous, widely published, quote:

> "The one concern of the Devil is to keep the saints from praying. He fears nothing from prayer-less studies, prayer-less work, prayer-less religion. He laughs at our toil, mocks at our wisdom, but trembles when we pray."

All these answers are wonderful and practical insights into what God has designed prayer to be, but they are by no means the only answers. It's interesting that God does not give us any one Scripture that clearly gives (at least in none of my gleanings of the Bible) only one definitive purpose for prayer. The infinite wideness of God and the immeasurable depth of His being — and His loving concern for the needs of people — allows many, many purposes for prayer's application. The more a believer's heart matures in prayer, the more it will be bent to align with God's will, His Word, and His agenda. And therein may be one of the major purposes of prayer: It is God the Father using the intercession of believers, all down through the church-age, to answer the prayer Jesus prayed the night before His crucifixion — that we "may be one" (John 17:21) with the Triune God in our affections, our purpose, our heart, our mind, our soul, and our will.

Let's pray we would realize that when we truly pray, it is perhaps the sphere where we are most in unity with the Triune God.

Father,

Our hearts long to realize all that prayer is. We'd like to wrap that answer up in a beautiful box with a big red bow and give it to every believer the day they are converted. But that's not how You have ordained for us to appropriate such a magnificent gift. We must learn it through diligent application. You reveal it through sorrows and trials and great personal need; maybe most of all through Your work in our hearts to make us yearn to know You and revel in Your presence.

Day 48

Know that the Lord has set apart the godly for himself; the Lord will hear when I call to him.
— Psalm 4:3

I call on you, O God, for you will answer me; give ear to me and hear my prayer.
— Psalm 17:6

Prayer is a vast subject in Scripture. It is also, in many ways, a vast mystery. Any believer who stubbornly persists in practicing prayer sooner or later bumps into several questions that threaten to stall their endeavors:

> How does God square up my prayers with His sovereign will? If He is going to do what He's going to do anyway, what is the need for my prayer?

> Why are there prayers that seemingly never receive answers?

> Why is persistent, disciplined prayer so difficult to practice? It seems everything in everyday life, even the demonic world, fights to interrupt it.

> Why are there times when we don't "feel like" God
> hears us?

The psalmist in the text above didn't waste time with these questions. He was firmly fixed on the truth that God *will hear* when he calls on Him, and when he calls out to Him, God *will answer*.

Don't fret over the questions You have about prayer. Many of them are answered as we go along. And some of them — because God is a sovereign God — will require us to not concern ourselves with matters too great and too awesome for us to grasp (Ps. 131:1). If we look at prayer through the whole of Scripture, we see that it is a golden thread woven into and throughout God's eternal purposes, whereby He uses the Spirit-led prayers of godly people to affect the whole tapestry of His eternal plan. When Daniel prayed to interpret Nebuchadnezzar's dream, for instance, he had no inkling of what the future would hold between himself and this monarch in God's eternal purposes.

There is enormous complexity to God's eternal plans — lots of moving parts. No wonder there are connections and ramifications beyond our line of sight — perhaps beyond our ability to comprehend. This is part of prayer's great mystery — all the questions notwithstanding. But "When God makes and carries out his plans," Marshall Segal has written, "He plans for us to pray." Why God would include us in His sovereign decrees and intervention in human affairs is beyond all comprehension; but He has. What an honor, delight, and responsibility.

Please pray that:

- We would never be discouraged in prayer because there are things about it we don't understand.
- The LORD would brand into our heart the absolute certainty that *He hears prayer, and He answers it.*

Father,

When we have total faith that You hear and answer our prayer, there is a sense in which the mystery of prayer is very exciting and enchanting. We can love the mystery of prayer! We can look at all of life in anticipation of answers totally outside our imagination — "God-size" answers; answers we can delight in; divine surprises, if You will. Help us not to get ahead of You, but completely rest in Your sovereign ways. Among Your people, may this attitude be the norm and not the exception.

Day 49

So what shall I do? I will pray with my spirit,
but I will also pray with my mind; I will sing
with my spirit, but I will also sing with my mind.
— 1 Corinthians 14:15

We must remember that the goal of prayer is the ear of God. Unless that is gained, the prayer has utterly failed. The uttering of it may have kindled devotional feeling in our mind, the hearing of it may have comforted and strengthened the hearts of those with whom we have prayed, but if the prayer has not gained the heart of God it has failed in its essential purpose.

— C.H. Spurgeon

Empty, stale, ritualistic and rote prayer is boring, but to "gain the ear of God" is not. Ascending to the throne of grace and taking our place in joint prayer with Christ and the Holy Spirit is, as Andrew Murray has said "the highest and holiest calling" any saint will know while traveling on this earth.

Among many other descriptions, prayer is the great treasure-house of the believer. Out of it comes power for ministry, wisdom for choices, blessing for others, fruitful lives, and great personal renewal and joy for us. Martyrs have found refuge in it and angels have been dispatched at its call. Why, then, is it so lukewarm in this contemporary Church?

Christian leaders suggest various answers to the question of why praying with Holy Spirit-wrought power is so scarce today, and there is truth to them all. But all opinions considered, maybe the answer is much simpler. Perhaps we don't pray with Holy Spirit-wrought power because we don't know how! The Church of this century seems to be lacking in both Biblical instruction on prayer and in modeling it. There is no remedy for this except to get back into serious study of the Word and allowing it to shape and direct our prayer life.

There is a certain paradox to prayer. Prayer results in spending much time in the Word; but spending time in the Word motivates prayer. One leads to and empowers the other. But both activities must be attended and led by the Holy Spirit. If He is not involved, we fall short of gaining the ear of God. We need the Holy Spirit to use the Word of God to instruct us and to motivate us for prayer. He can't do that if we don't give priority to reading it.

Let's passionately pray for the world-wide Church, our own congregations, our pastor(s), our leaders, our teachers, and ourselves that:

- We search the Scriptures to learn the principles that govern prayer and practice them.
- The Holy Spirit would enlighten our minds to pray with understanding, according to the Scriptures.

Father,

There's absolutely no substitute for the discipline of daily being in Your Word. Help us to make it the priority of our life — if we don't get anything else done in a day, we need to read Your Word and respond to it in prayer.

Father, we know Satan fears prayer. Would You protect us from his attacks that interrupt it?

"Satan can't keep God from answering our prayers, but he will keep us from asking."
— Adrian Rogers

Day 50

Let us not become weary in doing good,
for at the proper time we will
reap a harvest if we do not give up.
— Galatians 6:9

We don't like to wait. But most ministries involve waiting for a fruitful outcome. It takes time for planted seeds to germinate, take root, mature, and produce a harvest. Prayer is usually in that category. Occasionally God hears our prayer and answers it so fast it takes our breath away; but that's the exception rather than the rule. Generally, answers to prayer require periods of trusting, patient waiting.

We recognize this truth about prayer when the answer does not seem forthcoming. So far as we can judge, the request is Biblically aligned. Our motive is for God's glory, our faith is solid, we are praying in the name of Jesus. We consider our petitions in light of the promises of the Word. Everything seems in order, yet the answer is delayed.

In this case, thinking of prayer as the sowing of spiritual seed has a calming effect on us. Like the gardener who plants squash, checks to see if it's coming through the soil, places a wire fence to keep the rabbits out, watches the progress of the blooms, and expectantly follows the growth of the fruit — we wait for the certain outcome. We may poke around to see if there's any progress, but we wait for the LORD to move. We can remind Him of the request and tell Him we trust Him to bring it about; but we don't panic. We rest in His omniscient wisdom and judgment.

We can be absolutely certain of two things. (1) If we pray Biblically, *God hears and He answers*, and (2), no power in the principalities above or earth beneath *can thwart prayer.* Only eternity will reveal the spiritual harvest our prayer initiates. We may not see it for months, years, or decades. We may not even see the effect of our prayer in our lifetime; but the LORD will reveal it on the day He takes all things into account and rewards His servants.

David referred to the conquering Son in Ps. 2:7-8, yet the answer didn't come until the birth of Jesus in Luke 2. Isaiah prayed for God to rip the heavens apart and come down to rescue Israel (Is. 64:1-12), but his prayer will not be completely answered until the second coming of Christ and His triumph over the nations. The scope of Hannah's prayer in 1 Samuel 2:1-10 reached to the coming King and His kingdom; but it, too, won't be realized until Rev. 11:15 when the world's kingdom will become the Kingdom of God and His anointed, Jesus Christ.

There seems to be a pattern in Scripture concerning deferred prayer: the longer the wait, the more magnificent the answer. We can afford the delay.

Let's pray for the saints that:

- We patiently wait on God to answer prayer, knowing He can answer, when it comes, in a magnificent way!
- We cherish this waiting because we are in good company with some of God's most choice servants.

Father,

There is excitement in waiting for You to answer when we pray according to Your will and Your Word. We know that when the answer comes, the enjoyment will be sweeter and more wonderful because of the anticipation. Let us not get tired of waiting but pray persistently and with great faith for Your plans to come about.

Day 51

Moses and Aaron were among his priests,
Samuel was among those who called on his
name; they called on the LORD *and he answered*
them. He spoke to them from the pillar of cloud;
they kept his statutes and the decrees he gave
them. O LORD *our God, you answered them.*
— *Psalm 99:6-8a*

Here is an intriguing question to ponder: Is prayer more important than obedience, or is obedience more important than prayer? Said another way: Can the effectiveness of our prayers rise above our obedience to God? Or can our obedience be complete without prayer?

Psalm 99:6-8 links prayer and obedience together. So does Psalm 66:18:

> *"If I had cherished iniquity in my heart,*
> *the Lord would not have listened."*

Two of the three men mentioned in the text above are among those God recognized as model Old Testament intercessors — Moses and Samuel. They practiced prayer and obedience at the same time. This is certainly the ideal.

But back to our opening question. Which is more important — obedience or prayer? Certainly, prayer without obedience is hindered. But obedience without real, Spirit-led prayer is worse. It should make us mourn and weep and want to cast ourselves down, inconsolable; because obedience without prayer is dry, sterile, legalistic, powerless, joyless, loveless, isolated, and hardened. We have only a form of religion without sweet connection with the living, Triune God! How can we say we love Him with our whole heart, soul, mind, and strength — what Christ said was the greatest commandment — and be prayerless? We would be like the woman who legalistically remains loyal to much of her marital duty but refuses any consummating intimate physical union or sweet communion and companionship with her husband.

Far better to be continually confessing and repenting of our failure in the area of obedience and asking forgiveness, than to be distant and indifferent and cold and hardened toward the presence of Almighty God — satisfied to be unconnected to Him.

Let's pray for all believers, that we hold both
disciplines in tension — obedience to the Lord,
of course; but hot passion in prayer first.

Father,

May we be people of prayer! We remember the story of Mary and Martha. We remember that Jesus said Mary had chosen the better part — sitting at the feet of Jesus in rapt worship and love (Luke 10:38-42). We also remember that the church at Ephesus did just about everything right — but they had become loveless (Rev. 2:1-7). Jesus threatened to remove their lampstand for this. Father — would You help us give first priority to our communion with You? May we learn well that our relationship with You is everything!

147

Why does Jesus threaten the church at Ephesus with such harsh judgement if they don't repent (Rev. 2:2-5)? Most of this message to Ephesus is commendation. Ephesus has worked hard. They have persevered. They don't put up with wicked men. They have tested those who claimed to be apostles but were not. They have endured hardship and have not given up.

But there is one reprimand — serious and heavy. It is bad enough to tip the scales of evaluation. Ephesus has left her first love — the love for the Triune God and for each other. It's such a serious charge that, if there is no repentance, Christ threatens to remove their lampstand — that is, they will no longer be a genuine church, but just the pretense of one.

The message to Ephesus teaches us that there is no amount of dedication or hard work, or excellence, or bravery, or creativity, or education — not even doctrinal correctness! — that makes up for lack of love toward God. Not loving Him leads in only one direction — a widening spiral away from Him.

Not loving God inevitably gives birth — sooner or later — to idolatry. The void in the soul will not be denied. It will be filled with something — if not God, then a substitute for Him.

Father,

Help us to realize that if we are too busy to cultivate our relationship with You because we are too busy in ministry — we are too busy. Help us to cultivate the love relationship with You to the point of being besotted and enchanted and totally, continually satisfied with You. Amen.

Day 52

Therefore he is able to save completely
those who come to God through him,
because he always lives to intercede for them.
— *Hebrews 7:25*

We often form perceptions of Jesus from different parts of Scripture that mean a lot to us. A young woman I know lost her husband after a protracted and difficult illness that left her not only grieving, but physically worn out as well. But she told me the experience also left her with a comforting view of Jesus. She saw Him as holding His arms out to her in great compassion as the one who says, "Come unto me, all ye that labor, and I will give you rest ..." (Matt. 11:28 KJV). Others might see Christ as David pictured Him in the beautiful Psalm 23 — as the great Shepherd of the Sheep.

In the little verse of Heb. 7:25 we are given another glimpse of Jesus, another way of comprehending what He is to us. He is our Great High Priest. He saves us completely. The King James version says, He is able to save us "to the uttermost" (Heb. 7:25 KJV). That means His intercession is active in our lives right now — with our name and petitions attached. It never quits. It covers everything and flows into eternity.

Christians have often used a succinct phrase to sum up what Christ has done for us. We claim: "Christ — crucified, risen, and coming again!" There we have the Christian faith in a nutshell, they say. And it's certainly a good way to think. But if we are to see believers completely and utterly saved in all areas of their lives, if we are to help the Church comprehend, take part in, and avail themselves of Christ's continuing ministry working in our lives — right now! — maybe we should enlarge our thinking to seeing Him as:

*Christ — crucified, risen, **interceding**, and coming again.*

We need to have a fixed view of Jesus as intercessor. Jesus did not rise from the grave, dust His hands off, go to His reserved seat at the right-hand of God, sit idly by — and then watch from Heaven to see how things were going with all those inept followers He left behind. No! His seat at God's right hand is a seat of continual, day after day, night after night, century after century, advocacy for His people. Not just the big things. He takes note of even the details. There is comradery and partnership with Christ in our prayer.

Christ's intercession includes everything we bring to Him. All the needs and affairs of all His children; all the spiritual warfare we encounter; all the furtherance of the gospel into all the world; every heartache and care we cast on Him; every person we are burdened for; every plea for mercy and forgiveness; every attempt to obey Him; every trial we are enduring — He brings it all to the Father.

Oh, Church. We have a Great High Priest. What a wonder! Let's engage with Him in His never-failing pleading to Almighty God.

Let's pray that our perception of Christ would enlarge to see Him as our Great High Priest who continually, actively intercedes for us as we pray to the Father in His name.

Father,

As we are learning to pray, encourage us to see Jesus more and more in His high and lofty position as our great advocate and intercessor. He is there 24/7. He understands. He loves us and continues to be involved in our lives, even at this present moment. We thank You that we can pray in unity with Him, and we cherish this unspeakably intimate privilege.

Day 53

*These [various kinds of trials] have come
so that your faith — of greater worth
than gold, which perishes even though
refined by fire — may be proved
genuine and may result in praise,
glory and honor when Jesus Christ is revealed.*
— *1 Peter 1:7*

Our small group is currently praying for the family of a young man who jumped out of his father's car into fast-moving traffic and died shortly afterward, leaving his family devastated. We're also praying for the driver who hit him — a promising young man who had just been called to the position of senior pastor in a northeastern city. We shake our heads and ask the question, "How should we pray for such grief in the hearts of all concerned?"

All believers are praying for people who are suffering tragic accidents, pain, illness, financial difficulties, family dysfunction, job challenges, and a host of other human problems. It's hard not to fall into the habit of only putting these people on prayer lists, asking God to watch over them, give them relief from suffering, and be with them. *But we can do much more for them than that.* As we pray for them, let's overlay the petition for their temporal needs with spiritual intercession for their strength, encouragement, endurance, growth, and spiritual needs.

First Peter 1:7 tells us there are reasons behind the trials in the life of believers. They come so that our faith can be proved genuine — which is a critical process. Faith is a very valuable commodity. It's more valuable than refined gold. Refined faith results in "glory and honor and praise" when Jesus comes and is revealed as King of kings and Lord of lords (1 Peter 1:7-9). We want to persevere through the process well and to God's glory.

So, let's pray that the Holy Spirit's ministries may be evident to all people experiencing trial. Let's bring the situation to God and then pray that the Holy Spirit will:

- Assure them of God's Fatherhood.   Rom. 8:16
- Bear His fruit of "love, joy, peace" in their souls.   Gal. 5:22
- Give them continual hope.   Rom. 15:13
- Encourage them.   Acts 9:31
- Counsel them.   John 14:16-17
- Remind them of the words of Jesus.   John 14:26
- Give them a vision of the infinite sufficiency
  of God, even in the middle of their suffering.   2 Cor. 12:9

Let's pray for them amid their adversity (and our own!) that they might remember the LORD is their refuge and shield. He is their strength and their helper. He is the one who invites them to pour out all their troubles on Him — 2 Pet. 5:7. He is the one who does not allow them such a great trial that they are unable to endure it —but gives them a way of escape (1 Cor. 10:13). Pray that they sense God's presence in their lives, even in the darkest days, in sometimes miraculous ways. Pray that they do not fear or worry about tomorrow but trust the LORD. Let's bear one-another's burdens and take them to the throne of God.

Let's pray for all God's people in their times of trial that they will sense His presence through the ministries of the Holy Spirit.

And when hard times come to those who have not yet believed in Christ, let's pray they will come to Him, be willing to be yoked with Him, and learn of Him.

Day 54

Now to him who is able to do
immeasurably more that all
we ask or imagine, according to
his power that is at work within
us, to him be glory in the church
and in Christ Jesus throughout all
generations, forever and ever! Amen.
— Ephesians 3:20-21

The LORD not only can do immeasurably more than all we ask or imagine, but He very often does, especially in connection with His purposes.

There are lots of examples of this truth about prayer in Scripture. Daniel asked God to look favorably on Jerusalem which was left desolated by the Babylonians — and he got the blueprint for human history (Dan. 9:15-27). Hannah begged for a son — and got Samuel, the last of the judges and one of Israel's greatest leaders (1 Sam. 1:10-20). Jacob wrestled with the angel of the LORD, refusing to quit until he got a blessing — and his name was changed to Israel, "one who contends with God and prevails" (Gen. 32:22-32). Elisha asked for a double portion of Elijah's spirit — and got the ability to perform twice as many miracles as Elijah (2 Kings 2:9). The thief on the cross wanted to be remembered — and got Paradise with Christ that same day (Luke 23:39). The Israelites in slavery in Egypt cried to God — and they got Moses, with all the attendant miracles. Abraham asked God to fulfill His promise of a son — and got all the nations of the earth blessed through him.

The LORD's inclination, if we pray in line with Scripture, is to give us greater and better and more lavishly than we ask. It would be good if His Church would avail themselves of this generosity. We often pray with so little faith, so little confidence in Him, that we ask for far too little.

God wants to give us really big things. He wants to answer us in far-reaching ways that we hadn't thought of when we prayed.

What would it take for us to pray and get bigger things than we asked for? There are several answers to this question, but two of them are: *Pray for the purposes and promises of Scripture;* and *pray according to his* "power that is at work within us." That is, the power that comes from the indwelling Holy Spirit. *And when we pray this way, God will not only give us what we ask, He will give us* "immeasurably more than we ask or imagine" (Eph. 3:20).

Let's pray that we learn to pray with Christ's power that is within us. Then expect, watch, and wait for really big answers to really big requests.

Father,

Help us to have a vision that sees far beyond our own sight. We tend to see only what affects us directly and at the present moment.

Give us the ability to see all human history — clear into eternity — through Your purposes. One of the really big things we would like You to give us is a world-wide Church that is given to mature, Scripture-based prayer! Would You work in us to give us that?

Day 55

Call to me and I will answer you
and tell you great and unsearchable
things you do not know.
— Jeremiah 33:3

Scripture says a lot about prayer — IT SAYS A LOT ABOUT PRAYER.

If we were to go through the Bible — starting in Genesis — and use a yellow highlighter to mark every passage that either refers to, instructs on, gives insight into, details the surrounding circumstances of, records answers to, or IS prayer ... the sheer volume of marked verses would be more than surprising — it would be staggering.

We can draw three conclusions about this information and turn them into prayer requests for the world-wide Church, our pastor(s), our leaders, our teachers, and ourselves.

First, prayer is an enormously important topic to God. He spends a lot of time instructing us about it. He illustrates prayer, gives examples of it, and commands it.

Second, God's people down through the ages have been people of prayer. They have praised, worshiped, wondered, thanked, complained to, wrestled with, and dared to confront Him in prayer. They have sought God, cried out to Him, argued their cause to Him, reminded Him of His promises, and have poured out their sorrow, grief, and desires. They have prayed on mountain tops, in muddy cisterns, in the heat of battle, lying in bed at night, and amid exile. His people have prayed from within the anguish of severe trial, as well as during the ups and downs of everyday life.

Third, there is much to be learned about prayer. It is a life-long pursuit. Although the newest believer can pray, it is at the same time an expanding spiritual experience. Just as communication between parent and child starts with little words and little thoughts, our communication with the Master of the Universe starts simply but grows in mature interaction and understanding. The better we know Scripture, the more insight we have into the thinking of God and the more mature our prayers will be.

Let's pray:

- That as we read Scripture, we will notice just how much of Holy Writ is connected to prayer and it will encourage us to pray intelligently and diligently.
- That we will patiently pursue the art of prayer — knowing that it takes time and experience with God to learn it well.

Father,

We would like to learn that our first resource in facing all the circumstances of life is prayer. We want You to show us the same things You told Jeremiah he could obtain through prayer. We want to learn things we have not realized before. Help us to see that understanding the deepest, most complex questions of life is connected to calling on You! Because when we listen to You speaking to us in Your Word, the Holy Spirit illumines what we hear; and as we respond favorably to it in our prayer, there is spiritual growth and understanding — even to understanding the most complex of life's questions.

Father, may we develop a life-view that is a carbon-copy of Yours and patiently give time to developing the art of prayer.

Day 56

But Abram said, "O Sovereign Lord,
what can you give me since I remain
childless and the one who will inherit
my estate is Eliezer of Damascus?"
And Abram said, "You have given
me no children; so a servant in my
household will be my heir."
— Genesis 15:2-3

When we try to discern how many portions of Scripture are connected in one way or another to prayer, a good place to start is with God's promises to Abram (later named Abraham). There are three very far-reaching ones in Gen. 12:2, 3 and 7. First, God promises He will make a great nation through Abram; second, He promises all the nations of the earth will be blessed through his name; and third, He promises He will give Abram's offspring the land of Canaan.

But Abram can't see how any of this is going to happen: He does not have a son! Without a male heir to carry on his name, how is any of this going to come to pass? So, he takes the matter to God in Gen. 15:2-3. It's not even an outright request. Abram just reminds God of His promise, and God answers the cry of Abram's heart. He will have a son — the child will issue from his own body through the covenant relationship with Sarai — and the descendants from this son will be as difficult to count as the stars in the sky.

We should take note of an important pattern in prayer that occurs here and follows through the entire Scriptures: God makes a promise — He burdens the hearts of His children to pray for that promise — and He answers above and beyond and greater than anything they ever imagined when they prayed about it. Here's the pattern:

Promises — Prayer — Answers

God did give Abram a son — Isaac.
He gave Isaac two sons — Jacob and Esau.
He gave Jacob, the chosen of the two, 12 sons — they become the 12 tribes of Israel.

Through Judah, one of Jacob's 12 sons, the lineage of Jesus Christ came. And through Jesus, all the nations of the earth will be blessed — including US!

God's promises to Abram reach out beyond the nation of Israel to the Gentiles of the world. They, too, will become sons of Abraham by adoption. They are mentioned in the book of Revelation:

> *After this I looked, and there before me was a great multitude that no one could count, from every nation, tribe, people and language, standing before the throne and in front of the Lamb. They were wearing white robes and were holding palm branches in their hands.*
> — *Rev. 7:9*

Every time we follow the stories of any of these Abrahamic sons in the Bible, we are seeing answers to prayer that were initiated by the promises God gave Abraham. In fact, we see God's answers reverberate all through the rest of Scripture.

Let's carefully search the Scriptures for the promises — specifically watching for those made to New Testament believers — and pray for them expectantly.

Father,

May we get a firm handle on this critical pattern to prayer. You make promises — the Holy Spirit works in our hearts to pray for them — and You answer far beyond our expectations. May this even change the way we study Your Word, because we love and value Your promises to us. So, we are constantly on the look-out for them. There is tremendous power in praying for what You have promised.

Day 57

*During that long period, the king
of Egypt died. The Israelites groaned
in their slavery and cried out,
and their cry for help because of
their slavery went up to God.
God heard their groaning and he
remembered his covenant with Abraham,
with Isaac and with Jacob.*
— Exodus 2:23-24

God promised Abram three great, far-reaching promises: He will become a great nation: all the earth will be blessed through Him; and God is going to give Abram's offspring the land of Canaan. God had answered Abram's question about the first two by assuring him of Isaac's birth. But Abram has another question about the third promise. How is he going to know that he will inherit Canaan (Genesis 15:8)?

God responds to this latest prayer with one of the most spectacular visions in all of Scripture — He gives the Abrahamic Covenant. He pictures it with a blood covenant, something that was typical for sealing agreements in the culture of the day. He tells Abram to sacrifice a heifer, a goat, a ram, a dove, and a young pigeon. He was to cut everything in half except the birds. He was to arrange the pieces opposite each other on the ground. Then God puts Abram in a deep sleep and gives him a vision Israel will never forget.

> *As the sun was setting, Abram fell into a deep sleep, and a thick and dreadful darkness came over him. Then the Lord said to him, "Know for certain that Your descendants will be strangers in a country not their own, and they will be enslaved and mistreated four hundred years.... In the fourth generation Your descendants will come back here, for the sin of the Amorites has not yet reached its full measure." When the sun had set and darkness had fallen, a smoking firepot with a blazing torch appeared and passed between the pieces.*
>
> — *Gen. 15:12-13; 16-17*

In this vision, Abram and all Israel to this day see the symbols of God's presence pictured in the smoking firepot and the flaming torch. The smoking pot pictures the cloud that will lead Israel from Egypt to the Promised Land by day, and the flaming torch pictures the pillar of fire that will lead them by night. They see God's continual involvement with Israel pictured as He walks between the pieces of the sacrifices, because there's going to be a long interval between the promise and its fulfillment. They understand from Gen. 15 that God has 400 years of slavery in Egypt in store for them — but they also hear God's promise to lead them out to Canaan.

Israel sees all this come to pass. In Egypt they respond to their servitude with prayer. They cry out to God for help (Ex. 2:23-24). He hears them and He answers. *The entire book of Exodus* is the practical, detailed answer God gives Israel. Exodus includes everything from the call of Moses to lead them out of Egypt to Joshua leading them across the Jordan into Canaan. One could even argue that *Numbers and Deuteronomy* are the same, because they detail and rehearse everything that happened as God answered their prayers to bring them out of Egypt. *Leviticus,* too, has more to do with prayer than we might at first think.

Matt. 5:17-20 says that Jesus did not come to get rid of the Law; He came to be the fulfillment of it. Leviticus codifies the righteousness required of the perfect Lamb of God — and the perfect High Priest — who makes it possible for us to pray.

> Exodus, Leviticus, Numbers and Deuteronomy — that's four books of the Old Testament related to prayer. God indeed has a lot to say on the subject.

> Let's pray for the Church, that we begin to look for the continual thread of prayer that runs through the entire Bible; that we understand the enormous part intercession plays in God's purposes and we take our responsibility to pray for His promises very seriously.

Father,

It's a new revelation to us just how much of the Bible is connected to prayer. Father, we want to give it priority in our lives in the same proportion You do in Your Scriptures. Because prayer is critical to the fulfillment of Your plans, help us see the wonder of the part we can play in their fulfillment.

Day 58

But when they cried out to the LORD,
he raised up for them a deliverer,
Othniel son of Kenaz, Caleb's
younger brother who saved them.
—Judges 3:9

If we strolled around in a religious bookstore, we probably wouldn't find a lot of people standing in line to buy a study-guide written about the book of Judges. That is because some of the saddest words written in the Bible, and some of the ugliest stories, are in this book. But to the person interested in learning to pray, it is a goldmine of encouragement, because Judges is a book containing lots of prayer and its answers.

After the generation from Moses to Joshua passes on — despite all the miracles and all the wonders Israel had seen — the next generation falls far from God and commits some of the most heinous sins the Bible ever records. God brings judgment on them by allowing other nations to invade and conquer them, making their lives as miserable as anything they had seen under the Pharaohs of Egypt.

For about 365 years — the Period of the Judges —there is a cycle that occurs repeatedly. Israel falls into idolatry — God allows their enemies to conquer them — He can endure their misery no longer, and in answer to their cries, He raises up a judge.

Prayer is the key that summons God's help. In fact, we find the phrase, "they cried out to the Lord" (Judges 3:9) or some variation of it, over and over in the book. In this text, the nation of Aram is defeating them. They cry to God and He raises up Othniel, a relative of Caleb. Othniel goes to war and defeats Aram, and Israel has peace for forty years. Then the nation falls again into idolatry.

In Judges 3:15, three nations come against them. They cry to God and He gives them Ehud, a left-handed man. Ehud defeats the Moabites, the Ammonites and the Amalekites, and Israel has peace for eighty years. They endure with another judge, Shamgar, but after him, they again fall away from God.

In Judges 4:3, Sisera, a Canaanite army commander, has iron chariots and oppresses Israel for twenty years. Israel cries to God and He raises up a woman judge, Deborah. She sends Barak as general of Israel's forces. During the battle, a woman, Jael, drives a tent peg into Sisera's skull. With his death, his army is defeated, and the beautiful worship song of Deborah and Barak is recorded in Judges 5. Then Israel has peace for forty years.

In Judges 6:8-28, as they cry to God (vs. 6, 7) He sends a prophet, the angel of the LORD, and another judge — Gideon. We all know Gideon's story. He goes to war with only 300 men.

Samson, the son of a godly and praying man, appears before the nation falls almost entirely away from God. Even Jonathan — descendent of Moses — becomes involved in practicing idolatry (Judges 18:30-32). Things remain in this same situation until Hannah prays for a son in 1 Samuel 1:10-20 and God gives her Samuel.

There are two major points we should observe as we consider the book of Judges:

- Very clearly, on a very large scale, we see the pattern God so often gives to prayer: He promises something, He burdens people to pray for it, and He answers in great detail and power.
- God's willingness to answer prayer if we turn to Him in repentance and faith is always available — no matter how far we stray.

Let's pray that:

- We develop an enduring view of God that sees and worships Him as the promise-giving, prayer-answering, promise-keeping God of the Universe.
- We remember that it's a very short distance back to the Lord when we confess, ask forgiveness, and repent.

Day 59

I make known the end from
the beginning, from ancient
times, what is still to come.
I say, 'My purpose will stand,
and I will do all that I please.'
— Isaiah 46:10

Are you surprised that 6 of the first 7 books in the Bible detail events that answer prayers connected to the promises God gave Abraham in Genesis? It is a marvelous reality that God's purposes, His promises, and the prayers of His people are all sovereignly connected. Through them He brings all things to consummation. The Scripture is full of the details. Yet God gives additional promises that grow out of and further the ones He gave Abraham.

For instance, God reveals His purpose and promise to build a house for David — and David asks God for it to come about (2 Sam. 7:11b; 25). The history of David's descendants in 1 & 2 Kings, 1 & 2 Chronicles, and the linage of Christ in Matthew and Luke flesh out answers to this prayer in the practical events of life.

God reveals His purpose and promise to Jeremiah that the Babylonian Captivity will last only 70 years and then He will arrange to bring the exiles back to Jerusalem (Jer. 11; 29:10-14). Daniel prays for the fulfillment of the promise (Dan. 9:1-10), and the books of Ezra and Nehemiah record the events of God's answer.

God reveals His purpose and promises concerning the birth of Messiah in the prophetic portion of Isaiah 9:6-7. Simeon and Anna are two who cling to this promise and pray for its fulfillment. God sends Messiah Jesus, and the events of His coming occupy all four gospels in the New Testament — Matthew, Mark, Luke, and John all record the details of this story.

God reveals His purpose and promise to build a Church that the gates of hell can't overcome (Matt. 16:13-20), and believers are shown specific ways to pray all down through the years for this promise to become practical reality in the history of Acts and the epistles of Romans through Jude.

God revealed the promise, "I have installed my king on Zion, my holy mountain" (Ps. 2:6), and His people are to pray for it. Each time the Old Testament prophets beseeched God to set His Messiah as king in Jerusalem, and each time the Church prays on the topic of His Kingdom coming and His will being done, God is in the process of answering these prayers. And He gloriously answers them once for all in Rev. 11:15:

> The seventh angel sounded his trumpet and there were loud voices in heaven, which said: The kingdom of the world has become the kingdom of our Lord and of his Christ, and he will reign for ever and ever.

Let's pray that all believers would view prayer as their partnership with the Lord in bringing about His purposes.

Father,

We are beginning to see that in many respects, the entire Bible is permeated and flavored with prayer. It accompanies Your plans and promises as surely as heat accompanies fire. Give us eyes to see this truth and excitement to involve ourselves in pushing forward Your eternal program. We want our prayers to be included in the incense offered to You in Rev. 8:4. What a purpose for living!

Day 60

How Should We Now Pray?

When we realize how much God's purposes, promises and prayer are connected in Scripture, and how much Scripture speaks to the topic of prayer, we come to understand we're not limited to asking only temporal requests — that is, asking for things related to this physical, present world and its challenges. This aspect of prayer has its place, and we thank the Father for the opportunity to come to Him with our present needs; but we want to learn to be involved in His agenda and plans for our ultimate future. We want to pray, like so many of the Biblical intercessors, for the LORD's decreed purposes and promises to come to pass, too.

Father,

Would you hear us as we learn the habit of doing prayer like your saints in the Bible did? Help us to pray like David, like Isaiah, like Hannah, like Daniel, like Moses and so many others. Help us to see that this is not an impossible aspiration. It's very doable as we pray the Scriptures and rely on the Holy Spirit to enable us.

Psalm 32:6 says:

Therefore let everyone who is godly pray to You while
You may be found; surely when the mighty waters rise,
they will not reach him.

Father,

*We want Your people to be people of prayer. We want them to
read Your Word and respond by lifting it up to You and asking You
to fulfill what You have said, we want to pray this specifically for the
people in our own sphere of life (insert names). We want them to see
that when a troubled world rises against them, prayer is the major
avenue that lifts them far above the storms.*

John 6:35 says:

Then Jesus declared, "I am the bread of life. He who
comes to me will never go hungry, and he who believes
in my will never be thirsty.

Father,

*We want missionaries in hostile countries to be able to lay
out the Bread of Life in creative ways — to live the love and joy
of Christianity before the people there. Give (insert the names
of specific missionaries serving specific countries) opportunity,
boldness, and wisdom to speak the name of Christ and point to
faith in Him. We pray for our churches, too. We want them to find
their sustenance in Christ alone, and not turn to the things this
world offers as substitutes for Him. Deliver us from trying to find
what only You can give — and what only You can provide — from
something the world offers. You alone really satisfy our souls.*

Second Corinthians 4:17-18 says:

For our light and momentary troubles are achieving for us an eternal glory that far outweighs them all. So we fix our eyes not on what is seen, but on what is unseen. For what is seen is temporary, but what is unseen is eternal.

Father,

We want (name a specific person) to realize that the trials and difficulties they are experiencing right now may seem endless and hardly endurable, but the end is eternal joy. Help them to set their eyes on You, get their strength from You, find a refuge in You, and realize what is seen is soon passing away, but what is unseen lasts forever. Let them sense Your presence and be comforted and encouraged.

In the name of Jesus, the name above all names — Amen.

For the earth shall be filled with the knowledge of the glory
of the LORD, as the waters cover the sea.
— Habakkuk 2:14 KJV

Day 61

*If ye abide in me, and my words
abide in You, ye shall ask what
ye will, and it shall be done unto You.*
— John 15:7 KJV

Here are some interesting questions to contemplate: What is the supreme best thing we can do for the world-wide Church? What is the best thing we can do for our pastors, our leaders, our teachers, our congregations, and ourselves? What is the best thing we can do for our marriages, our children, our friends, our mission endeavors, and everything else encompassed in Kingdom work? What is the best thing we can do for hurting, suffering people?

We could list many answers to the questions above, but the supreme answer might, even in a book on prayer, surprise us.

Charles Spurgeon called John 15:7 the "golden key to prayer." Here are some excerpts from his sermon, *The Secret to Power in Prayer*:

> The Lord gives the abider *carte blanche*. He puts into his hand a signed cheque, and permits him to fill it up as he wills.

Does the text mean what it says? I never knew my Lord to say anything he did not mean. I am sure that he may sometimes mean more than we understand him to say, but he never means less ... .

It is to a certain class of men who have already received great grace at his hands [the abiders] — it is to them he commits this marvelous power of prayer. O my dear friends, if I may covet earnestly one thing above every other, it is this: that I may be able to ask what I will of the Lord and have it ... One such man as this, or one such woman as that in a church, is worth ten thousand of us common people. In these we find the peerage [royalty] of the skies ... .

God will put his omnipotence at Your disposal: *he will put forth his Godhead to fulfill the desires which his own Spirit has inwrought in You.* I wish I could make this jewel glitter before the eyes of all the saints 'till they cried out, "Oh, that we had it!"

... How clear it is that if we abide in Christ, and his words abide in us, we may ask what we will! For we shall only ask what the Spirit of God moves us to ask; and it were impossible that God the Holy Ghost and God the Father should be at cross-purposes with one another. What the one prompts us to ask, the other has assuredly determined to bestow.

[emphasis added]

The best thing we can do in all situations is to abide (remain) in Christ; that is, be constantly connected to and living in Him, and allowing His words to live in us because this is truly the golden key to effective prayer.

Pray for the world-wide Church, Your own pastor(s), Your leaders, Your teachers, Your own congregations, and Yourselves that:

- We would learn to abide (remain) in Christ and allow His words to abide (remain) in us.
- We would treasure this abiding relationship with Jesus — it is the most important thing in our lives.

Father,

One of the surprising things You teach us when You show us how to pray is that relationship with You is everything — not only for our own lives, but for the effectiveness of our prayer in the lives of others. Ah, Father! When the sorrows and suffering and needs of others overwhelm us, it is crucial we be on rock-solid praying ground so that we can intercede for their great need. They desperately need Your divine intervention.

Help us to understand that the moment-by-moment interaction with You in trust and obedience is critical to prayer! Help us to understand and practice the concepts of walking through life hand-in-hand with You, of doing life with You, and of being constantly aware of Your presence.

Day 62

The prayer of a righteous man
is powerful and effective.
— James 5:16b

Moses was a man who fit the definition of an effectual fervent intercessor. At least three times he stands between Israel and complete judgement because God was so angry with their idolatry and disobedience, He threatened to destroy the whole assembly and start over. At least three times Moses interceded — once during the episode with the golden calf in Ex. 3, once when they refused to enter the promised land in Num. 14, and again at Korah's rebellion in Num. 16. Not only that, but once in intense battle, Moses prayed — and as long as he held up his arms beseeching God, Israel prevailed over Amalek.

Elijah was a man of effectual fervent prayer, too. He prayed and a widow's son was raised from the dead (1 Kings 17:17-24). He prayed for rain after a three-year drought (1 Kings 18:41) and God poured rain on the land of Israel.

John Knox was a James 5:16 man of prayer. Mary Queen of Scots feared him so much she said, "I fear the prayers of John Knox more than the combined armies of Europe."

Can we be people of effectual fervent prayer, too? What is it going to take for 21st century Christians to pray that kind of prayer — prayers that stay God's hand in judgment, prayers that stop armies, prayers that change people's lives, prayers of which the world takes notice? Do we think it possible? The truth is, it's probably simpler — although not easier — than we think.

God tells us in the New Testament the parameters within which we may ask Him for anything we will — and He will give it to us. Effective, fervent prayer that accomplishes a great deal, for instance, has to do with praying in Jesus's name and being in the John 15:7 abiding relationship. It is connected to bearing genuine fruit because of this relationship, asking in faith, and being willing to deal with the sin the Holy Spirit convicts us of when we are praying. It's concerned with asking according to God's will and genuinely wanting His glory.

Do these seem like difficult conditions for prevailing prayer? That's a good question.

But a better question to ask, by far is: Is prevailing prayer worth the effort to follow these guidelines? We will never reach them all perfectly — but we certainly should strive to reach them genuinely. One writer has very perceptively written:

> It is far easier for the flesh to submit without the answer [to prayer] than to yield itself to being searched and purified by the Spirit until it has learned to pray the prayer of faith.
>
> — Andrew Murray
> *With Christ in the School of Prayer*

May we want answers to prayer more than we want our own ease.

Let's pray that we would be willing to do what we must do in order to pray effectively; that we would yield to the Holy Spirit's probing work in our hearts, because it is part of the process that brings us to effective praying.

Father,

Would You work in us — in the circumstances we live in — in the people who have influence on us — in the trials we encounter — so that we are willing to learn to pray as You show us? Help us to see that effective prayer is worth having at any price. Open our eyes to the possibilities and power available to us through it.

Day 63

*He has delivered us from such
a deadly peril, and he will deliver
us. On him we have set our hope that
he will continue to deliver us, as you
help us by your prayers. Then many
will give thanks on our behalf for the
gracious favor granted us in
answer to the prayers of many.*
— *2 Corinthians 1:10-11*

It is only a few days from the close of 2020 as I put this entry into the final manuscript of this book. It's been a year of great upheaval and challenge in American history. Because of Covid-19 and political unrest, the entire world seems a boiling cauldron, threatening to overflow at any moment. From now until the Lord returns, the Church is going to be involved in these events and their consequences.

Pastors are faced with these global events and their effect on their congregations. The sheep are being attacked from every direction, especially the media. This calls for informed, Spiritual-war-focused prayer from their people.

Let's pray for our own pastor(s) and all those who faithfully preach the gospel of Jesus Christ clear to the ends of the earth that:

- God would give them wisdom to lead their churches, in light of the events and evil worldviews currently espoused.
- He would give them courage to stand for truth despite popular lies.
- He would work in them to major on the essentials of ministry and eliminate the frivolous.
- He would allow them to see the emphasis on prayer that needs to be taught and modeled in their congregation.
- He would allow them to understand that persecution could well be in their church's future, and they should prepare their people to face it.

Let's pray very closely aligned with 2 Cor. 1:10-11 for all those on the front-line of ministry — especially pastors, that:

- God would protect them from peril.
- We would help them by our prayer.
- We would thank God for the blessings granted to our pastors through our prayer.

Father,

We don't know all the details, nor the exact sequence, of what the future holds for Your Church and its leaders; but we do have a general idea of things to come. We sense we are living in perilous times as the second coming of Jesus is drawing closer, and we want our pastors, leaders, and people to be prepared.

We trust You for the future. Help us to refuse to go down the path where fear leads; but to go down the path where faith in You and

Your Word leads. We recognize these two paths go in two different directions to two different destinations. The path where fear leads is a very dangerous and destructive place.

Please don't allow our pastors, leaders, and people to be tempted beyond what they can deal with but give them a way out (1 Cor. 10:13) and deliver them from all evil. We know this plea needs to be a continual prayer for them and for ourselves.

Day 64

———————— *But Moses sought the favor of the Lord* ————————
his God. "O Lord," he said, "why should your
anger burn against your people, whom you
brought out of Egypt with great power and
a mighty hand? Why should the Egyptians
say, 'It was with evil intent that he brought them
out, to kill them in the mountains and to wipe them
off the face of the earth'? Turn from your fierce
anger; relent and do not bring disaster on your
people. Remember your servants Abraham, Isaac
and Israel, to whom you swore by your own self:
I will make your descendants as numerous as the
stars in the sky and I will give your descendants
all this land I promised them, and it will be
their inheritance forever.'" Then the Lord
relented and did not bring on his people
the disaster he had threatened.
— Exodus 32:11-14

Exodus 32:11-14 relates a pretty gutsy thing: Dust is arguing with Deity!

Let's look at the details of the account. Moses is interceding for Israel after God has pronounced His intended judgement regarding Aaron's golden calf. God fully intended to wipe Israel out for this sin and start over again with only Moses.

Theologians might have varying opinions on this striking response from God. But one thing is completely clear from this passage: God relented and changed His intended course of action in response to the intercession of one pleading man.

In his book *Purpose in Prayer,* E.M. Bounds writes:

> "The more praying there is in the world the better the world will be, the mightier the forces against evil everywhere. Prayer, in one phase of its operation, is a disinfectant and a preventive. It purifies the air; it destroys the contagion of evil."

Again, Bounds says, "God shapes the world by prayer." We would probably have little quarrel with that statement if, (1) we consider the Great High Priestly prayer of Jesus in John 17, and if, (2) we understand Christ's advocacy at the right hand of God. Because of these two truths, believers today have an incredible privilege. With their prayer, they are indeed involved in God shaping the world. They can take part in the same kinds of work Christ did — in multiplied instances all through the Church Age. Jesus said in John 14:12:

> *"I tell You the truth, anyone who has faith in me will do what I have been doing. He will do even greater things than these, because I am going to the Father."*

Moses had the courage to stand between God's judgment and the nation of Israel. In spite of all the aggravation and headaches they gave him, he must have loved them enough to use every argument at his disposal to save them from the judgment of God. Do we love the Church and the world around us enough to do the same?

Let's pray that we would learn to argue God's promises as Moses did, because we are asking for the sake of His name and are concerned with His glory.

Father,

John 14:12 is one of the Scriptures that always confused me: How could we ever do more and greater works that Jesus did? Help us to be aware of the countless ways the Church can do the same kind of works as Jesus — and in greater and greater numbers — because we pray down the intervention of Your omnipotent hand on the world we live in today.

Day 65

For God, who said, "Let light shine out
of darkness," made his light shine in our
hearts to give us the light of the knowledge
of the glory of God in the face of Christ.
But we have this treasure in jars of clay
to show that this all-surpassing power
is from God and not from us.
— 2 Corinthians 4:6-7

Have you ever marveled at your own salvation? Isn't it a wonder that God enabled us to respond to His spiritual light in our hearts so that we comprehend the brilliant, heavy weight of God's worth because it's been revealed to us in Christ?

But verse 7 points out another wonder: We have this treasure in physical, decaying bodies ("jars of clay"). As long as we live in this present world, we are a *redeemed soul residing in a yet to be redeemed body.* Scripture refers to this spiritual reality when it talks about the new self that is contained within the *old self.*

You were taught, with regard to your former way of life,
to put off your old self, which is being corrupted by its
deceitful desires; to be made new in the attitude of your

minds; and to put on the new self, created to be like God
in true righteousness and true holiness.
— *Eph. 4:22-24*

We could illustrate this spiritual reality with a simple picture:

The "old man" with self on the throne of the life.

> The redeemed "new man" with
> Christ on the throne of the life.
> 2 Cor. 5:17

[Eph. 4:22-24]

We are born into this world with an unregenerate nature that has self at the center of our lives — represented by the larger rectangle. Sometimes called the natural man; it is spiritually dead, blind to spiritual truth, and corrupted in its desires. But at salvation, we are created anew (2 Cor. 5:17) where the Holy Spirit, represented by the smaller rectangle, takes up residence. He produces His fruit (Gal. 5:22-23) and performs His ministries in us. The Holy Spirit makes us spiritually alive, opens our eyes to spiritual truth, and replaces our corrupt desires with righteous ones.

All believers struggle with the desires of the old person — the physical "jars of clay" (2 Cor. 4:7) which is a poetic name for the physical flesh. It conflicts with the desires of the new, regenerate person, no matter how Young or how mature we are in the faith. We must choose which voice we will listen to and heed — the voice of self, or the voice of the Holy Spirit of God. Our prayer is greatly affected by this choice.

Let's pray that we refuse the desires and influence of the old person and respond to the guidance of the indwelling Holy Spirit.

Father,

We are aware every day of the continual conflict between the flesh and the new person that we are in Christ. No matter how much we long to walk in the new person, our flesh rises up at the slightest provocation — especially in the areas of the self-sins: self-protectiveness, self-indulgence, self-promotion, self-defensiveness, plain selfishness, etc. Strengthen us, we pray, to overcome these tendencies. Help us to do what the old Puritans called "mortifying" the flesh. That is, say NO to it and put Biblical responses in place to whatever the issue of the moment happens to be.

Day 66

You were taught, with regard to your former way of life, to put off your old self, which is being corrupted by its deceitful desires; to be made new in the attitude of your minds; and to put on the new self, created to be like God in true righteousness and holiness.
— *Ephesians 4:22-24*

Here is an illustration of what Ephesians 4:22-24 is talking about: Before I was married, I worked in the offices of a large aluminum plant. The girls in these offices organized a social club where they did things together outside work. They had a bowling league, for instance, and planned weekend outings to Pittsburgh or Washington D.C. to see plays, stay overnight, and spend the next day shopping. I sometimes took part in these activities. But after my marriage, there was a change. I was now in an important new relationship that radically affected how I chose to spend my weekends.

One of the realities of the Christian life is that we come into an *eternally* radical new relationship that affects our choices. It is no longer just us residing in our soul: The Holy Spirit of God comes into us and lives in us. We find ourselves experiencing conflict between the old self and the new self. The Holy Spirit speaks into our hearts according to the Word of God and woos us to follow His leading, which is to do life with Christ. But the old self is continually enticed to listen to and follow the world's opinions, our own desires, and the lies of the evil one, which is to do life according to the flesh.

At any given moment, believers are doing one of two things: Either we are putting on the new and putting off the old, or we are putting on the old and putting off the new.

That is, we are either listening to the Holy Spirit and making choices consistent with His leading, or we are refusing to listen to and heed the Spirit, thus putting off Christ and choosing to walk according to the dictates of the old self.

How wonderfully patient God is with us in this struggle. The LORD does not overwhelm us. Our choice to walk with Jesus — to put off the old and put on the new — is always a *present-tense, one thing at a time, decision point.* We are always faced with these choices, one after the other. We wake up in the morning — do we get out of bed and spend some time with the Father in His Word and prayer, or do we hit the snooze button and go back to sleep? We hear an unflattering story about someone — do we get on the phone and spread it around, or do we refuse to assassinate their character? We're tempted to buy something we don't need and can't afford — do we buy it regardless, or do we follow the Spirit's guidance and practice self-control? The flesh pulls us one way, and the Spirit of God pulls us the other. Who will we heed?

Let's pray that we listen to the still, small voice of the Spirit and follow His leading in the choices of our lives — even in our thoughts, motives, and intentions, as well as our outward actions.

Father,

The fact that You commit Your own omnipresent Spirit to come dwell in us is a wondrous, unfathomable reality! How can we ever fully comprehend it?! Surely, this realization should tremendously help us in deciding who we will listen to and follow — the Spirit or the flesh. These are vital decisions, because if we're not habitually walking in the new creation where God is on the throne of our lives and the Spirit resides, there will be times when we're not praying in the Spirit either.

Day 67

Response to putting off the "old man"
and putting on the "new,"
(Eph. 4:22-24) which is an important
concept in the practice of prayer.

There's an old proverb about several blind men describing an elephant. One touches the elephant's tail and says an elephant is like a snake. Another touches the elephant's ears and says the first man is not right: An elephant is like a flat, flapping sail. The third touches the elephant's leg and says the others don't know what they are talking about. An elephant is like a tree trunk, and the fourth, trying to push against the elephant's side, says they are all wrong: An elephant is like a high, stout wall that nobody can move. The truth is, the blind men needed an over-all view of the animal before they could even begin to describe it accurately.

This proverb helps us understand why God often teaches us spiritual truth by giving us several viewpoints of the same concept — so that we can comprehend the whole. We need to be able to see the entire "elephant," so to speak.

Scripture uses several terms — nearly synonymous, yet slightly different — that complement and complete the action of putting off the old and putting on the new.

One of these terms is "Walk in the Spirit" (Gal. 5:16 KJV). This is

194

another one of the conditional promises: If You walk in the Spirit (putting on the new), You won't be fulfilling the desires of the flesh (putting off the old). The idea is to walk through life in step with, listening to, and obeying the leadership of the Holy Spirit rather than our own desires.

Another term is *sanctification*, which is the process by which God sets us apart to be like Christ, not just in principle, but in action. In Jesus's prayer of John 17:17, He asks God to complete this process through His Word. We effectively put off the old man and put on the new one as we conform to what the Word teaches.

The last term is one we encounter a lot when we talk about prayer. It is John 15:7, where Jesus says to remain (live) in Him and let His words remain (live) in us. It is the *abiding principle*; the living relationship Jesus illustrates by referring to a branch in living relationship with the vine. Both actions demand the abandonment of the old person in a practical way. We can't live in Christ and live in the flesh at the same time; we can't have the words of Christ directing us and the words of the flesh directing us at the same time. We must choose to put off one in order to put on the other.

So, these additional concepts help us comprehend what Ephesians 4:22-24 is talking about when it speaks of putting off the old and putting on the new:

Walking in the Spirit — going through life in step with the Spirit of God Who works in us.

Sanctification — Our cooperation with the Spirit of God as He takes us through trials and lessons in order to set us apart as belonging to God.

The John 15:7 relationship with Christ — like the living relationship which is illustrated by a branch remaining fixed in the vine.

Father,

Help us comprehend these teachings and see them as different points of view on the same precept. It's a hard truth to discipline ourselves to, but how we live totally affects our prayer life! If we are out of step with the Holy Spirit most of the time, fighting His work in us to set us apart for You, content to live separated from Christ and His words, and often enjoying living in the old man, prayer is often a futile, lifeless exercise and we can't really expect much from it. Deliver us from such spiritual sloth.

Day 68

Do not be anxious about anything,
but in everything, by prayer and petition,
with thanksgiving, present your requests
to God. And the peace of God, which
transcends all understanding, will guard
your hearts and your minds in Christ Jesus.
— Philippians 4:6-7

Ever since a period of great trial in my life in 1993, these two verses in Philippians have made the page they are written on the most used page of my Bible. Hardly a day goes by that I don't need to be reminded to step out on their promise and trust what they say.

Some of the promises in Scripture are unconditional. For instance, Acts 1:11 declares Jesus is coming again. This is unconditional — it's going to happen, and it doesn't make any difference what anyone does to try and stop it. On the other hand, there are many, many *conditional promises* in the Word. A few of them are:

> *"Come to me" (the condition) — "and I will give you rest"*
> *(the promise):* Matt. 11:28
> *"Call to me" (the condition) — "and I will answer you"*
> *(the promise):* Jer. 33:3

"Give" (the condition) — "and it will be given to You" (the promise): Luke 6:38

God has given His people a prescription/promise for personal peace — spiritually, emotionally, and intellectually. But it is a conditional promise. There are some things required of us, as indicated in Phil. 4 verse 6 before we can appropriate it.

When anxiety grips our heart, the condition is for us to replace it with prayer and supplication, which is a natural response of believers; but it is to be prayer immersed in, saturated with, wrapped up in, and flooded with *thanksgiving.*

When anxiety reaches the point where we feel like rolling on the floor for relief, God's will for us is to take Him at His word in the conditional promise of Phil. 4:6-7. We can step out in faith on that promise and pour our needs out to Him, then thank Him for everything from the shoes on our feet to the eternal inheritance we have in Him — and everything we can think of in between.

I remember a Navigators' missionary who once told me we can't control the emergence of our emotions — they are physiological responses that arise unbidden from what we think about. But we can control what we think about. And as we do, our emotions come under control. The beauty of Phil. 4:6-7 is that when we are thankful, we are allowing God and His presence in our lives to control what we think about. Our eyes move away from our problems and become fixed instead on the great Problem Solver. He brings unexplainable peace to our hearts and minds.

Let's pray that:

- We refuse anxiety — and when it surges up in our hearts, we replace it with going to the Lord in prayer — with lots and lots of thankfulness to Him.
- We thank God for His peace, marveling that it is beyond human understanding.

Father,

We understand, though, that practicing Phil. 4:6-7 is not a one-time fix for anxiety's hold on us but is an act of faith that needs to be practiced daily all through our lives. Thank You that when we mingle our prayer with thanksgiving, it produces the marvelous peace we so desperately need. We can trust that Your answers to our cares will be perfect answers. We love the sense of being "tethered" to You.

Another Thought on Conditional Promises

Is it possible that many promises in Scripture lie dormant until they are activated by prayer, that they lie unclaimed in our lives? Of course, this is true! Because many of the promises are conditional and believers neglect or refuse to meet the conditions.

Ah, Father,
Ah ... Father!
As we read the Scriptures, we can't help but notice that the vast majority of Your promises are conditional. Even the salvation promises require something from us. For instance:

That if You confess with Your mouth "Jesus is Lord," and believe in Your heart that God raised him from the dead, You will be saved (Rom. 10:9).

... that whoever believes in him should not perish, but have eternal life (John 3:16).

Father, help us not leave Your thousands of promises unclaimed, dormant, inactive, and unappropriated because we neglect to meet the conditions! Help us in our day to realize how desperately we need what You have promised to us, Your Church, and be willing to step out on the conditions.

"Nothing before, nothing behind;
The steps of faith fall on the seeming void, and find the Rock beneath."

— John Greenlief Whittier

Day 69

*My prayer is not for them alone.
I pray also for those who will believe
in me through their message, that all
of them may be one, Father, just as you
are in me and I am in you. May they
also be in us so that the world may
believe that you have sent me.*
—John 17:20-21

In the opening chapters of Genesis, we see God reveal to us three major Biblical themes that will be fleshed out, illustrated, and explained through the rest of the Bible:

1. God created people for a love relationship with Himself, which glorifies Him greatly.
2. Sin destroyed that love relationship, which, if not restored, will result in destruction, death, and judgment.
3. But the restoration of the love relationship with the Triune God will be made possible, explained, enlarged, expanded, and made glorious *for believers* through the sacrifice of the "Lamb of God," Jesus Christ.

All of Scripture continually moves forward with these themes in view. The LORD uses common, everyday events, actions, characters, and objects in the Bible — marriage, families, kings, seedtime/harvest, storms, sacrifice, heroes, fruit trees, war, etc. — so that we will have greater illustration of what God is doing as He is bringing this restored relationship about. We understand Christ as the coming king, for instance, because we know the position kings have held in our world. The common and physical help us understand the spiritual and eternal.

There are several supplications Jesus makes to God the Father in John 17 the night He was betrayed, and the Father is in the process of gloriously answering them all. But the supplication we are most interested in in this entry is the spiritual reality of one-ness with the Triune God (John 17:20, 21). Christ asks that God give us a wondrous spiritual gift: That all believers be brought into the same circle of relationship that God the Father, God the Son, and God the Holy Spirit have always had from eternity past. God answers this prayer, and it is a *fabulous* privilege! How can I explain it in this short devotion? It would take several books of theology to fully explore. But perhaps all we really need to know is this: God the Holy Spirit is in the believer; the believer is in Christ; and Christ is in the Father. At salvation, we are brought into this intimate circle of unity.

What a privilege the believer has when they can see and understand all of history from the perspective of this glorious unity. It is the one-ness Christ refers to in John 17:20-21 that makes possible the intimate, warm, loving, companionable, sweet, and satisfying relationship with the Triune God we so yearn for. Truly, nothing short of that relationship with Him will ever eternally satisfy the human soul. "You have made us for Yourself, O Lord," Augustine wrote, "and our hearts are restless until they rest in You."

Let's pray that:

- We would praise and worship God the Father who brings us into the circle of the same relationship He has always had with the Son and the Holy Spirit.
- We would be overwhelmed with the realization that on the night He was arrested, *Christ prayed for us as individuals.*

Father,

What a marvel! You created us to have a love relationship with You, the Triune God, and Jesus prayed for US as individuals the night He was arrested and on His way to the cross. May we never get over these wonders. May they be sweet truths that we ponder, and hide, and treasure in the depths of our souls.

Day 70

Let us, therefore, come boldly unto
the throne of grace, that we may obtain
mercy, and find grace to help in time of need.
— Hebrews 4:16 KJV

Here's a splendid paradox of prayer: We are to come to the LORD with humility (Phil. 2:3-5), yet we are to come to Him boldly. We often think boldness and humility are mutually exclusive — if we have one, we can't have the other. That may be the case with humility and pride, but not with humility and boldness. These two should walk hand in hand in the believer's heart, especially regarding prayer. Humility is produced when we humble ourselves and boldness is produced when we exalt Christ.

Our invitation to come boldly to God in prayer is based on the fact that Christ is our sympathetic Great High Priest who has suffered the same things we deal with. He knew the pain of rejection from those who should have loved Him. He knew the betrayal at the hands of a friend. He knew hunger and thirst and the power of the devil to tempt. He knew excruciating physical pain during the hours of the crucifixion. And He knew separation from the Father.

Prayer affects a spectrum that is wide and deep. On the one hand, God includes the prayer of His people in the working-out and culmination of His plans and purposes — and we are certainly to ask for the

204

Lord to bring them about. But on the other hand, He condescends to help us in the cares of our lives. There can be no doubt that material needs have been met, prodigals have been restored, healing has been provided, worries have been eased, rescue has been enacted — and thousands of other practical day-to-day helps have arrived as praying people have brought their problems to God. What a privilege! We can come boldly in prayer and find the grace we need in the trials and difficulties of life. There is tremendous peace and comfort in bringing things that are too heavy, too big, and too difficult for us to handle to the attention of the all-powerful, all-wise God of the universe. There is nothing too big or too small.

There are no relationships outside the scope of prayer — no person outside the influence of it. Someone we love may show no interest in spiritual truth; may even be hostile to it. Their lives might not show any outward evidence that God is working in them. But He is working in answer to prayer. Or there may be a difficult person in our lives who continually creates havoc. God can change them, He can change us, or He can change or eliminate the situation.

Praying for help when we need it is in accordance with the will of God. He has instructed us to pray for it — and to do it boldly. We may have to wait some time for the answer, and when it comes, it may not be in the form we expected — but God has promised to hear when we ask for His help.

Let's pray that we would come boldly in prayer, asking God for His help in all needs; that we would wait confidently, knowing the Sovereign Lord is working in response to prayer.

205

Father,

Sometimes it is hard to see Your involvement in the lives of others when we pray for them — especially when we can't see any outward changes. May we be firmly convinced that when we pray — You work. Encourage us from Your Word regarding this.

"Expectation is the child of prayer and faith."
— C.H. Spurgeon

Help us, Father, to develop holy expectation when we pray.

Day 71

You do not have, because You do not ask God.
— James 4:2b

"The greatest tragedy in life is the prayers that go
unanswered because they go unasked."

— Mark Batterson, author of
*The Circle Maker: Praying Circles Around
Your Biggest Dreams and Greatest Fears*

It may very well be that the greatest sin of the contemporary church is prayerlessness — if not the greatest sin, then the greatest folly. Because if we are neglecting prayer, we are neglecting the proffered hand of Almighty God to intervene in this dark, sad, hopeless, floundering world we live in.

Christ is faithfully at His post! He's at the right hand of God, advocating and interceding for the saints. But where are the penitents? Where are the pleaders? Where are the intercessors? Where are the worshipers?

Spurgeon was often asked the secret to his ministry. To which he often replied, "My people pray for me." Don't we know that those who preach desperately need us to pray for them? They need the penitents — the pleaders — the intercessors — and the worshipers — to toil in the bowels of the ship and stoke the fires that put flame under their preaching. They need men and women in their congregation who mean business and pray prevailingly for them.

God help us to never, ever be guilty of prayerlessness. May we *have* precisely because we ask. And may we avail ourselves of Christ's advocacy and intercession. May we never *not* have because we do not ask God.

Pray for the world-wide Church, our own congregation, our pastor(s), our leaders, our teachers, and ourselves:

- That God would wring our souls with the need for prayer.
- That He would allow us to realize we often don't have because we don't ask!

Father,

We confess our prayerlessness. We get wrapped up in the affairs of life and don't give prayer priority. We confess that we waste a lot of time, too. Just the hours we spend in media participation every day would probably shock us. We are ashamed of this neglect.

Forgive us. We want to ask with the persistence of needy, desperate children.

Day 72

Is any one of you sick? He should call the
elders of the church to pray over him and
anoint him with oil in the name of the Lord.
And the prayer offered in faith will make the
sick person well; the Lord will raise him up.
If he has sinned, he will be forgiven.
— James 5:14-15

These two verses were very confusing to me when I first tried to understand prayer. If they were true, why didn't all the sick people we pray for get well? I remember a pastor in California, a very godly man, and the son of the Pastor Emeritus in our church. He had a rare, but deadly form of cancer. Our church prayed earnestly for his healing, but it was not to be. The LORD took him home. Were we not praying with enough faith? Did we fail to go through with the right way to anoint oil? Why did God not raise him up, like James 5:14-15 promises?

John MacArthur's commentary on the book of James (pages 276-278)[2] helps a great deal in coming to terms with these verses, and I highly recommend reading it. MacArthur refers to James 5:14-15 as the

---

2 The John MacArthur New Testament Commentary James ©1998 Moody Press/Chicago, ISBN: 0-8024-0900-8 quoted by permission.

"most misunderstood and disputed portion of this passage." He writes:

> "It is true that, apart from the present verse, *astheneō* is translated sick eighteen times in the New Testament.... . But it is also used fourteen times to refer to emotional or spiritual weakness.... . Significantly, in all but three [of the fourteen times] (Phil. 2:26-27; 2 Tim. 4:20) of *astheneō's* appearances in the epistles it does not refer to physical sickness. Paul's use of *astheneō* in 2 Corinthians 12:10 is especially noteworthy, since it there describes weakness produced by the sufferings of life — in a similar context as its usage in the present verse."

> "The weak are those who have been defeated in the spiritual battle, who have lost the ability to endure their suffering. They are the fallen spiritual warriors, the exhausted, weary, depressed, defeated Christians."

> "The wounded, exhausted, broken sheep are to go to their shepherds, who will intercede for them and ask God for renewed spiritual strength on their behalf."

> "Through the righteous prayers of godly men, God will restore His battered sheep's enthusiasm."

The Scripture does not promise to heal and restore every physically sick person we pray for. God often *does* graciously heal them in response to our prayer, but not always. Although we can, and should, petition Him for those with physical illness or injury, like other petitionary prayer, we must accept that sometimes He says yes, sometimes He says no, and sometimes He says wait. We make the petition, and then would be wise to exhibit the same attitude as Jesus when He asked for the cup of the crucifixion to pass from Him — "Nevertheless, Thy will be done" (Luke 22:42 KJV). We may grieve deeply at the loss of someone we love, but our loving heavenly Father knows best — we can trust His choice.

Let's pray for those who are in a spiritually weakened state because of the suffering produced by trials — prolonged illness being one of them. Let's ask that the LORD restore them to spiritual vitality and heal them of physical sickness if it is within His will to do so.

Father,

Help us to rest in You and trust Your love and wisdom when a sick person we are earnestly praying for passes from this earth. We can rest in Your providential care.

Day 73

*Then he said to his disciples, "The harvest
is plentiful, but the workers are few.
Ask the Lord of the harvest, therefore,
to send out laborers into his harvest field."*
— Matthew 9:37-38

We are certainly living in a harassed world in this present day. People are confused, hurting, and searching in every direction hoping to find meaning, truth, and inner satisfaction. What's going to fill this void in their lives? The voices of the world suggest lots of different answers for them — like money, fame, success, position, pleasure. The world promises these things will surely be the answer. But at the end of the day, when the pursuit of these superficial substitutes for God don't fill the hungering soul, people pursuing them are left like a thirsty man adrift on the ocean: There's water all around him, but the more he drinks seawater, the thirstier he gets.

People desperately need to hear the invitation of John 6:35:

> *Then Jesus declared, "I am the bread of life. He who comes to me will never go hungry, and he who believes in me will never be thirsty... ."*

Jesus is the spiritual bread that gives life and the spiritual water that satisfies. But people can't come to Him until, by some means, they hear about Him. Matt. 9:36-38 gives us a direct command. We are to pray for workers to take the good news of salvation in Christ, and then work to disciple those who believe.

In this confused, hurting, God-denying world, people are longing to find answers. They need to hear the good news and they need to see believers whose lives reflect Jesus Christ. They need to see us loving each other, denying ourselves, giving of ourselves, and practicing the Sermon on the Mount in our relationships. They need Christians who are willing to be involved in their lives.

The world needs to know that the one who delivers from sin and death and hell and fills the void in their souls is Jesus Christ. We are to pray for God to send someone to tell them.

Please pray for the world-wide Church, that we pray earnestly for God to send workers to the mission fields.

Father,

Help us be willing to plant, cultivate, or harvest wherever You call us. Give us lasting fruit from this labor. If we aren't called to go to a foreign mission field ourselves, help us to financially support the work and remember missionaries on the field who have labored years to break up hard ground so the seeds of the gospel can be sown. Help us be faithful to stay in contact with them and pray for them — they need our encouragement.

Day 74

I want to know Christ and the power of
his resurrection and the fellowship
of sharing in his sufferings, becoming
like him in his death, and so, somehow,
to attain to the resurrection from the dead.
— Philippians 3:10-11

Philippians 3:10 is a familiar verse. Commentaries have a lot to say about it. We can read them and teach them and pass on their insight to others. We can find out the Greek words and what they mean, and many fine sermons have used this verse for their text.

But it is in prayer that we really comprehend and *experience* the spiritual depth of this verse.

The disciples talked to Christ every day. They walked with Him. They shared His good times and his bad times. They observed His miracles and His life. They had daily knowledge of Him. We think of them as very privileged to have done so. We wish we could have been there.

But New Testament believers have opportunity far beyond, greater than, deeper than, and more powerful than the disciples' 3-year earthly experience. We are privileged at any given moment to enter the presence of the glorified Christ — where He "always lives to intercede for them [us]" (Heb. 7:25) and do business with God.

Do we realize that prayer takes us out of the realm of academics? It moves us away from the distant, the theoretical, into the warm, passionate, alive, throbbing, person-to-Person interaction with Christ. We are brought face-to-face with the Triune God! Do we comprehend that it is in prayer we become truly like Him in his death — given over to the great purpose for which He died? That we actually share what He suffered for, that we actually take part in and claim the power of His resurrection, in our own lives and in the lives of others? That as we intercede with Him day after day, we come to know Him in a way that is up-close and personal? He's not just the Son of God that we worship from afar — a little unknown and intimidating — but the God-man at our side! The apostles had seen and heard, and their hands had touched Christ (1 John 1:1). We can't do that physically. But in prayer we do it spiritually. We experience a relational one-ness with Him and are critically involved with Him in bringing in His Kingdom.

O, believer! Do we sense His presence? Do we, like Esther, see the golden scepter extended to us as we enter the presence of Almighty God — because we are in unity with Jesus Christ, the one we join in His continual intercession for the saints?

The Triune God bids us to the seat with Christ in the Heavenlies. It is up to us whether we will enter in or stay away.

Let's pray for the world-wide Church, our own congregations, our pastor(s), our leaders, our teachers, and ourselves that:

- We would "know Christ and the power of his resurrection and the fellowship of sharing in his sufferings, becoming like him in his death" (Phil. 3:10).
- We would revel in and delightfully enjoy our fellowship with Him as we pray.

Ah, Father,

This is what we long for in the prayer experience! We want far, far more than the dry, academic, and theoretical. We want passionate interaction with YOU! We want to know You, to share Your suffering, to see Your resurrection power in our lives and the lives of others. We want to unite our purpose with Christ's purpose in His death. Show us how to pray like this!

Day 75

After consulting the people, Jehoshaphat
appointed men to sing to the LORD and to
praise him for the splendor of his holiness as they
went out at the head of the army, saying: "Give
thanks to the LORD, for his love endures forever."
— 2 Chronicles 20:21

We should never underestimate the value of praise in prayer. It reminds us of who God is and what He can do, and it is great indication of our faith in Him. We see the worth of praise in the story of Jehoshaphat, king of Judah and sixth in the line of kings descended from David.

Jehoshaphat was a good king. He proves the sterling character of his faith in the story of 2 Chronicles 20:1-30. At the beginning of the chapter, Jehoshaphat receives the message that three armies are marching to attack him. Knowing he humanly can't win against the combined armies of three countries, He calls a fast throughout Judah and goes to God in prayer. He ends his prayer with the words:

"O our God, will you not judge them [the enemy armies]?
For we have no power to face this vast army that is
attacking us. We do not know what to do, but our eyes are
upon you." (2 Chron. 20:12)

God responds to the prayer and speaks through one of the Levites, a descendant of Asaph. He tells Jehoshaphat that the battle is God's, not his. He tells him where the armies will be arriving, and to march out Judah's army against them — but they will not even have to fight.

Jehoshaphat obeys in a beautiful and touching act of faith — He marches toward the battle with his army and spears and javelins, their bows and shields and helmets: but their front line is a *singing choir, giving thanks to God before His promise to rescue them ever actually occurs.*

What a risk Jehoshaphat was willing to take! And what faith he displayed! We can learn a deep lesson from him. *The testing of real faith takes place in the crucible.* Anyone can trust God when things are going well and there are no dead ends. But when we have no other options, when no human help can suffice, when faith is left unpropped — naked and shivering and we can't see the deliverance — that's the time to step out in obedience.

God heard Jehoshaphat. He did what He so often does in His children's battles — He turned the enemy armies to fight against each other. By the time Jehoshaphat and his army got to the battlefield, nothing remained but bodies and spoils. All the kingdoms around Judah saw how the Lord fought for His people, and Judah had peace.

Let's pray that:

- When we are in trouble, like Judah during the days of Jehoshaphat, we bring our problems to God and praise Him lavishly.
- We step out in obedience and give thanks when we can't yet see the deliverance.

Father,

It takes a heart full of faith and obedience to march into life with praise on our lips when things all around us seem to be falling apart. Help us to see the value praise has in our prayer life. If we took all the prayers recorded in Scripture and separated out the amount of praise in them — it would be a very significant percentage of the whole. Help us to make sure our prayer is never without praising You.

Day 76

*Then Jacob prayed, "O God of my
father Abraham, God of my father
Isaac, O Lord who said to me, 'Go
back to your country and your
relatives, and I will make you prosper,'*
— Genesis 32:9

One of the ways that God teaches contemporary believers to pray is by recording and preserving the prayers of His saints in Scripture. One of these prayers is contained in Genesis 32:9-12. It is a prayer Jacob offered up amid a very difficult situation in his life when he didn't see any way out. It is short, but if we take it apart, we can learn principles that are a good template for our own prayer amid fearful times.

Jacob is in a tough situation. God is telling him to go back to his own country, despite the wrong he had committed against his brother Esau. He is on his way, but as he thinks things over, he decides to send a message to Esau, hoping to smooth things over and be received favorably. But when the messengers return, they tell him Esau is coming to meet him with 400 men! Things do not look good.

Jacob is afraid. It drives him to prayer — a good response for all of us when we find ourselves in tough situations. So, what does Jacob ask for in this critical moment?

First, Jacob approaches God and points out relationship with Him: He speaks of the LORD being his grandfather's God, his father's God, and the one who told him to return home to his own people.

Second, Jacob reminds God there was a promise attached to this instruction. God had told him He would prosper if he went back. So now Jacob is doing what God told him to do, and he finds himself with a big problem on his hands.

Third, he admits he does not deserve God's help, but thanks Him for the safety and prosperity he has enjoyed for the last 20 years —which was the answer to a vow/prayer he had offered up as a Young man on the trip as he fled from Esau in the first place (Gen. 28:20-22). It's interesting that Jacob does not get to the point of his need until after he goes over these three issues with the LORD.

Finally, Jacob makes his request. He asks the LORD to save him *and the children along with their mothers* and reminds God that He has promised to make his descendants as uncountable as the sands of the sea (Gen. 32:11-12).

When life's situations make us afraid, a good template for the prayer of New Testament saints is:

- Remember and express our relationship to God through Jesus Christ — that He is our Father.
- Recount the promises of Scripture — God's promises vanquish fear.
- Admit how helpless and undeserving we are, but express thanks for the blessings of the past.
- Tell the LORD what we need — then rest in His coming answer.

Father,

Jacob's prayer reminds us that You repeatedly tell us not to fear. It is the opposite of faith. But Father, we are reassured that coming to You when we are experiencing fear is a wise thing to do. It's okay to bring it to You. What's not okay is when we give in to fear and make choices motivated by it. Jacob didn't turn around and run back to Laban but waited on You to guide him through the situation. Help us continue following You even when we are afraid.

Day 77

Pray without ceasing.
— *1 Thessalonians 5:17 KJV*

It used to be a saying that mothers and teachers had "eyes in the back of their heads." That is, even if busy with some other tasks, they were continually aware of and engaged in everything going on around the children in their care. Is that the idea of this short verse in 1 Thessalonians — that we be joyfully and continually aware of prayer and engaged in it no matter what other task is occupying us at the moment?

Or does it mean New Testament believers should hold on to the doctrine of prayer, never letting it pass from Christian experience? Or is it suggesting a readiness for prayer that is continually in our soul? A devotion to prayer that characterizes our life?

The NIV translates this phrase in 1 Thess. 5:17 as, "pray continually." But is that even possible? For many years — I'm ashamed to admit — even as a believer, I passed over this verse because it did seem impossible to me. And even worse, praying without ceasing did not really seem very desirable. I did not enthusiastically pursue it nor understand the value of such a state.

The meaning of 1 Thess. 5:17 may be a combination of all the aforementioned ideas: an awareness and engagement of the soul to speak to God, whatever we are doing; a doctrine the church should hold in high esteem and never neglect; an inclination of the heart to turn and speak to God as we walk along with Him in life; a devotion to the practice of prayer and an unceasing response to Him in worship and praise and wonder.

If we understand the combination of all these ideas and see them modeled in the Scriptures as we read — praying without ceasing is not a difficult, impossible, distasteful concept. Actually, it is a very desirable state to be in! We can enjoy life with the Triune God and be in continual communion and communication with Him. We can avail ourselves of the wonder and power of His presence. We can affect spiritual, and even physical, affairs. We can dispel gloominess and the power of evil. What's not to like about that?

I remember once painting a picture of a birch tree beside a stream. My paintings were painfully amateurish, but this one turned out fairly well. I was pleased with the composition and subject. Yet there was something wrong. I wanted a picture of a pleasant summer afternoon, a restful place where someone would want to stop and put their feet in the water. What I got was a gray, dreary afternoon with the possibility of a storm just out of the picture. Then I realized what was wrong. There was no sunshine anywhere! So, I mixed a golden yellow glaze and applied it lightly over the entire painting. It worked beautifully. I wanted an afternoon drenched with sunshine, and the glaze did the trick. It gave me exactly the feeling I wanted to convey.

Like that picture, when we are in the attitude of continual prayer, it puts a spiritual golden glaze of the presence of God over everything we see. Prayer literally lights up our lives!

Let's pray for the entire world-wide Church that:

- Our hearts and our souls will be in continual prayer-readiness mode.
- We would never neglect the *doctrine* of prayer in our assemblies — that we would teach its structure, principles, scope, its possibilities, and privilege — that we would model it well before our people; that it would be a part of our regular sermons.

Father,

Forgive us for our reluctance to pray continually. Help us see that it is a holy habit that pays wonderful dividends. May we walk along in life consciously aware of Your presence, enjoying You, and ready to speak to You in prayer with only the fraction of a moment's notice.

Day 78

*"When anyone wrongs their neighbor
and is required to take an oath and they
come and swear the oath before your
altar in this temple, then hear from heaven
and act. Judge between your servants,
condemning the guilty by bringing down
on their heads what they have done,
and vindicating the innocent by treating
them in accordance with their innocence.*
— *1 Kings 8:31-32*

Believers, it's impossible to reason with evil. We can't co-exist with it, saying, "You stay on your side of the fence, and we'll stay on ours." We can't compromise with it or make some kind of treaty with it or ignore it. Evil presses forward, consumes, destroys, and never backs down. The only solution to it is justice and judgment.

This portion of Scripture in 1 Kings 8 is one of the first petitions Solomon asks of God in his prayer at the dedication of the temple. Not surprisingly, it is a plea for God's involvement in enacting justice and judgment, because Solomon knew a society cannot long endure without them.

Justice and godly judgment are not popular ideas in modern culture.

226

But they are prominent themes in the Bible, all the way from Gen. 1:1 to Rev. 22:21. Adam and Eve were judged justly; Cain was judged; the people of Noah's day were judged; Israel in the desert was judged. Even Christ's crucifixion was a judgment, because God justly judged sin at the cross for all those who put their faith in Jesus, the perfect Lamb of God. The last book in the Bible speaks of the Great White Throne Judgment (Rev. 20:11-13) where those who have rejected Christ are judged for what they have done in this life.

But despite how fearful judgment is, we must remember that real justice is not possible without it. Peace in a culture cannot flourish without it. We may never have thought of it, but "everlasting righteousness" (Daniel 9:24) — one of the decreed promises Daniel received regarding the end of this age — cannot possibly come in without judgement and justice, because evil would just keep coming back.

Without justice and judgment, God would cease to be completely what He is, because His attributes would be incomplete also. He would lack the authority and power to carry through on His promises and decrees. If He were not a just God, we could no longer trust Him to remove evil and establish righteousness.

Let's pray for the world-wide Church that:

- We do not relegate God's judgment of sin to the pile of unnecessary doctrine.
- We make sure both God's justice and His judgment are concepts included in our teaching and evangelistic messages.

Father,

Help us to never depart from the doctrine of just judgment. Help us see that it is not a negative truth, but a very positive, life-giving, holy value. Help us see that the doctrines concerning judgment play a huge part in conviction and repentance.

Day 79

But I [Jesus] tell you: Love your enemies
and pray for those who persecute you,
that you may be sons of your Father in
Heaven. He causes his sun to rise on the
evil and the good and sends rain on
the righteous and the unrighteous.
— Matthew 5:44-45

Maybe one of the most difficult instructions Jesus gave us on how to pray is contained in these two verses. We are to love, and we are to pray for our persecutors. When we see how the persecuted Church is treated — slandered, property confiscated, forced marriage, denial of food and other necessities of life, imprisonment, and unspeakable torture — our flesh rises up in anger. But the Lord calls us to another response.

It helps us to love and pray for our enemies and persecutors if we remember their terrible condition. Their minds can't understand spiritual truth. They are excluded from life in God (Eph. 4:18). They have eyes, but can't spiritually see; ears, but can't spiritually hear. The precious words of the Spirit of God seem foolishness to them (1 Cor. 2:14). They have terrifying judgment ahead of them when they stand before God; and when Satan whispers in their heart, they have no defense against him. Our period of their persecution will be short; but their punishment for such sin will be eternal.

Remember, the Apostle Paul was a persecutor before He came to faith in Christ.

Remember, we may be the only person — ever! — who prays for these persecutors.

Remember, the only gospel they may ever encounter is our love and prayer for them.

Remember, the reward for obeying the Lord and praying for our enemies and our persecutors will be huge:

> *Blessed are You when people insult You, persecute You and falsely say all kinds of evil against You because of me. Rejoice and be glad, because great is Your reward in heaven, for in the same way they persecuted the prophets who were before You.*
> — *Matthew 5:11-12*

There are several references to the reward of the persecuted. For instance, Smyrna, the persecuted church in Rev. 6:11, is one of only two churches that receive no reprimand from the Lord Jesus — only reward. 2 Cor. 4:14 refers to those who suffer for the name of Jesus when it says, "For our light and momentary troubles are achieving for us an eternal glory that far outweighs them all." Romans 8:18 says what we are suffering in this present time can't begin to compare with the eternal heavy weight of worth (glory) that we will receive when we are with God. Persecution is for a short time; but we reign with Christ for eternity.

Let's pray for all those who endure persecution because they bear God's name, that they will be comforted and protected; that their faith does not fail; that they receive God's grace to love and pray for their persecutors.

Father,

We read of the sufferings of Your Church in many parts of the world and are appalled. But help us, by Your grace — when we pray for the persecuted believers — to pray for their persecutors as well. This is beyond any human inclination; it can only be done in Your strength. But it is pleasing to You, and we want to show ourselves to be Your children.

Day 80

Put on the full armor of God so that you
can take your stand against the devil's schemes.
— Ephesians 6:11

Evil is very real and very persuasive. Whether as believers we are aware of it or not, the devil's schemes are at work all around us. Satan is the ultimate liar, murderer, destroyer, and supplanter. As we press toward the coming of the Lord, we must contend with him daily. How do we do that? How should the Church in this day go about fighting in spiritual arenas?

When we fight spiritual forces, we are to use spiritual weapons. The Bible describes the weaponry we need for spiritual warfare. It is: "truth", "righteousness", "the gospel of peace," "faith," "salvation," and "the word of God" (Eph. 6:10-20 KJV).

We armor up by embracing God's truth — especially with Christ, who IS truth. We reject lies — anything contrary to Him. We work hard to live a lifestyle of godliness and heartfelt obedience to the Lord. The centrality of our message is always salvation through the life, death, and resurrection of Jesus — salvation by grace and through faith in Him. We believe what God says and use it as a defense shield that we hold up to repulse Satan's attacks. We develop our thinking based on what God's salvation has done for us; and we use the Word of God to go on the offensive against all evil.

Once our armor is in place, what do we do? Evangelize? Teach? Disciple? Minister? Preach? Yes — all those things: But the first thing we are to do — before we attempt any of these actions — is to pray. Six verses after we see the armor listed, we see the instructions to use it.

> *And pray in the Spirit on all occasions with all kinds of prayers and requests. With this in mind, be alert and always keep on praying for all the LORD's saints. Pray also for me, that whenever I open my mouth, words may be given me so that I will fearlessly make known the mystery of the gospel, for which I am an ambassador in chains. Pray that I may declare it fearlessly, as I should.*
> — *Ephesians 6:18-20*

It is a mistake to attempt evangelism, teaching, discipleship, ministering and preaching without time spent at the Mercy Seat beseeching God for the power to *use the weapons we have donned.* It is said that E.M. Bounds, a chaplain during the Civil War who wrote books powerfully exhorting the Church to prayer, whose books are still mined today for their wisdom, himself prayed three hours a day before he ever wrote a word.

We may not be able to dedicate that many hours a day to prayer, but we can give it first priority in our day. We are living in days equally perilous to E.M. Bounds' time — probably even more so as we see the day approaching when the Lord comes back. The battle calls for spiritual armor and the serious practice of prayer.

Pray for the world-wide Church, that we put on the whole armor of God, then recognize prayer as the *first* assault on the forces of evil in this world. Pray that we be disciplined and dedicated to it.

Father,

May donning Your armor not just be a Sunday School story to us — but may we take it as deadly serious, because it is. Eternal issues and the ability to fight evil is in the balance for our churches, our communities, and our children. Let us remember that Daniel's prayer was a component of angelic warfare. (Dan. 9:20-23)

Day 81

*At Gibeon the LORD appeared
to Solomon during the night in a
dream, and God said, "Ask for
whatever you want me to give you."*
— 1 Kings 3:5

Football is my favorite spectator sport. It is a game where one team attempts to cross a goal line with a football in their arms. They are opposed by a team of 245-pound gorillas who stand between them and the goal and are determined to stop them.

Of course, there are rules. For instance, a team has four chances to advance the ball ten yards. If they can't, the ball is turned over to the other team. A defender can't grab his opponent by the face mask. A team can only have eleven players on the field, and they must line up to start the play correctly, etc. *Contenders win only if they play within the boundaries of the rules.* Break the rules and the referee stops the play with his whistle.

This same concept applies to what we could call the Great Conditional Prayer Promises of the New Testament. In 1 Kings 3:5, God gave Solomon the right to ask Him for anything. Do you wish God would tell you the same thing? Do you want to pray for God to work in someone's life — and He does? Do you want to pray for deliverance from some impossible to overcome situation — and the LORD grants you

235

just that? Do You want the Father to tell You the same thing He told Solomon, giving You the invitation to ask for whatever You want Him to give You? Well, God has told New Testament believers exactly that!

One of the most tremendous realities of prayer is that there are at least seven places in the New Testament where God gives us the promise of receiving what we ask for — but they are conditional promises. In other words, we must pray within the boundaries of the conditions.

The conditional prayer promises — if viewed as the boundaries of prayer — *are the most powerful weapon available for Christ's Church, next to the Word of God itself.* When we pray within them, we can literally ask God for anything, and He has promised to give it to us. The answer comes in His time and in His way — but the promise is sure.

We will talk about these conditional prayer promises for the next seven entries because there is no more valuable information on prayer in this book.

If a football team wants to win, it must play within the boundaries of the rules. If we want God's promise to give us whatever we ask, we must pray within the boundaries of the great conditional prayer promises.

Father,

We can't imagine what would happen in this world if Your Church could receive from You anything they ask. The possibilities of this kind of prayer should excite the most lethargic saint!

We've got to admit, though, we have some questions about the concept. How does it work? We've experienced getting some of the things we've asked for in prayer — but receiving anything we ask? In all honesty, LORD, we haven't seen very much of this kind of prayer in our own lives, nor can we say we've seen it in the lives of very many other believers, either.

But we can't argue with Your Word. You definitely make these promises — so why are we not more confident of Your answers? Help us to understand, Father. We want You to show us how to pray.

Day 82

*In that day You will no longer
ask me anything. I tell You the
truth, my Father will give You
whatever You ask in my name.*
— John 16:23

The first conditional prayer promise is that we ask in Jesus's name.

Passwords are a fact of life in this computer era. We can't access anything on-line without them, including automated teller machines. One rainy evening, I was in a hurry to get to a meeting but decided to run through the bank. I pulled up to the ATM, put my card in and typed what I thought was my four-digit code. I was wrong. The machine blinked a couple of times and spit out my card. I had money in the bank, but there was no access to it without the password.

In one sense, *the name of Jesus is the password* that gives access to Almighty God in prayer. But praying in His name is not a kind of mantra with mystical power which we verbally tack on to the end of prayer so God will hear us. Praying in Jesus's name is not about a phrase we use, it is about utilizing the right Jesus gave us to *use His name* when we approach God in prayer. The name of Jesus always merits Almighty God's attention.

In another sense, praying *in the name of Jesus is like having check-writing privileges on His bank account.* But there is stewardship responsibility attached. God does not give us this privilege so we can fulfil our selfish desires. We are to use His resources within the context of His purposes — to further His will.

But in the greatest sense, *praying in Jesus's name is having our own personal recognition of the superiority and majesty that God has imbued in Christ's name.* We are cognizant of *who He is and what He has done —* He is the "only divinely promised, given, and accepted burnt offering ..." (CHS) for our sin, making our salvation possible — and we *enter prayer worshiping because of it.*

Names have great significance to God. They are carefully chosen to represent the character, the accomplishments, the position, the identity, and the worth of the named one. We are to deeply **reverence** the name of Jesus when we pray.

> *Therefore God exalted him to the*
> *highest place and gave him the name*
> *that is above every name;*
> *— Philippians 2:9*

We must realize that we have no merit on our own to enter God's throne room: *God hears us because we come in the name of Jesus — as Christ's representative; praying under the auspices of His power, authority, position, and approval.* May we never abuse this privilege. Our attitude for prayer that always receives a "yes" should always indicate we have a clear understanding of these truths.

Pray for the world-wide Church, our own congregation,
our pastors, our teachers, our leaders, and ourselves that
we would understand, utilize, and thank Jesus for the
right He has given us to use His name in prayer.

Father,

We know this is just the first of the conditional prayer promises, but it's not difficult to understand. We love having access to You through the name of Jesus, and are greatly encouraged, for if You hear Jesus, You hear us. We also love having "check-writing" privileges on His unlimited resources.

But we have to confess, so many times we neglect the reverence for His name that You intend. We cheat Jesus of our worship when we do this. It includes a name so great that Rev. 19:12 says only He, Himself, will understand it. Help us remember that reverence for Jesus's name is critical to meeting the conditions of John 16:23.

Day 83

*If You remain in me, and my words
remain in You, ask whatever
You wish, and it will be given You.*
—*John 15:7*

The **first** conditional prayer promise is John 16:23-24.
Ask in Jesus' name.

The **second** is John 15:7. We are to remain in Jesus and
His words are to remain in us.

John 15:7 may be the greatest of the seven conditional prayer promises because the other six are the products produced from it. It is a part of Scripture where Jesus uses a very common illustration to show us the necessity of a vital, living relationship with Him in our prayer life. He compares this relationship to a fruit vine. He is the vine, and we are the branches. He is wanting us to see that, just as the branch is in living connection with the vine — receiving the life-giving sap that flows through it and produces fruit on the stem — we must be in a living connection to Him by taking in His Word and allowing it to do its work in us. Remaining in Christ means *we are in the Word* (taking it in consistently), and the *Word is in us* (effectively changing and directing us as He is in us).

Does John 15:7 mean, then, that we can ask absolutely anything and God has obligated Himself to give it to us? The answer is yes — *if we are meeting the conditions of all 7 of the promises.* These conditions should not discourage us, they should tremendously *encourage* us — simply because the opportunities to meet them are freshly offered to us every moment of every day! We can't change the past — its opportunity is gone; and the future is not here yet to impact: but we can choose to seize the present.

Our *remaining in Him* and *His Word remaining in us* is not a static, unchanging state. It's not something we finally accomplish and then it stays in place for the rest of our lives. It fluctuates. At any given moment we are either remaining in Him and His Word remains in us, or we are NOT. It is a present-tense choice.

Simply put, are we absorbing the Word? Are we being reminded of it by the Holy Spirit? And are we believing and submitting to whatever it says — *in the present moment* when the Holy Spirit brings it to mind? If we are, we are fulfilling the conditions of John 15:7. We may not be practicing John 15:7 perfectly, but the more we make present-tense choices to practice it, the more effective our prayer will be.

Let's pray for the Lord's Church, that we daily remain, moment-by-moment, in Christ, taking in the Word and responding to it as the Holy Spirit leads.

Father,

It's becoming clearer to us that our understanding of prayer has somehow, over the years, become far removed from what You mean for it to be. We've missed the warmth and intimacy and relationship of prayer — the closeness of walking hand-in-hand with Jesus. You are Almighty God, and You live "in unapproachable light" (1 Tim. 6:16). You are the sovereign King of the universe — and we understand that even though You are our Father, we need to approach You in reverence. But we are so glad that when (1), we come to You in the name of Jesus, and when (2), we are remaining in Him and His words are remaining in us — we are beginning to put ourselves in position for You to give us whatever we ask for in prayer. There's more to learn, we know; but these two precepts go a long way to educate us in the art of effectual prayer.

Day 84

*You did not choose me, but I chose you
to go and bear fruit — fruit that
will last. Then the Father will give
you whatever you ask in my name.*
— *John 15:16*

The **first** conditional prayer promise is John 16:23-24. Ask in Jesus's name.

The **second** is found in John 15:7. Ask remaining in Him and His Word in us.

The **third** is in John 15:16. Ask as a fruit-bearing believer.

One Christmas I saw a beautiful plant called a "holly fern." It had tiny holly-shaped fronds and was covered in bright red berries. I brought it home and gave it the place of honor in our bay window. Over time, the fern began to shed leaves. I was concerned, but the berries still looked plump and healthy, so it was probably just getting acclimated to my house. But one morning I walked into the living room and the holly fern looked crispy-crunchy. Nearly every leaf had fallen. I was left with a skeleton plant covered in bright red berries.

Puzzled, I began to examine the plant more closely and made a terrible discovery. The berries were fake fruit! They were little, red-painted plastic balls that had been wired all over the plant.

What does Jesus mean by bearing fruit? He is talking about obedience to the instructions of the Word of God that results naturally in fruit produced from our living relationship with Him. At salvation, our heart has been changed, and obedience is not about following rules. It is about the acts resulting from our connection to Him. Apple trees bear apples; palm trees bear coconuts; raspberry vines bear raspberries; and those in Christ bear *Christ-like behaviors.* Any good produced in our lives because of the John 15:7 relationship is a fruit. This covers a lot. What we think, what we do, what we say, our motivation to act — if it is initiated by our relationship with the Lord, it is fruit.

Christ is, among other things, talking about the fruit produced by the indwelling Holy Spirit. Gal. 5:22-23 KJV speaks of them — "But the fruit of the Spirit is love, joy, peace, long-suffering [patience], gentleness, goodness, faith, meekness, [self-control]; against such there is no law." As we yield to the urgings of the Holy Spirit, we produce His fruit.

Phil. 1:11 refers to the fruits that righteousness produces; that is, making Christ-like choices amid life's dilemmas, and Heb. 13:15 KJV refers to offering up "praise to God continually, that is, the fruit of our lips giving thanks to his name." There are varying degrees to which believers produce fruit. The good soil, in the Parable of the Sower (Matt. 13:18-23) produces fruit — sometimes 30 times what was planted; sometimes 60 times, and sometimes as much as 100 times.

But while it's true that some believers produce more fruit than others, if we are to claim the conditional promise of John 15:16, we must be bearing some amount of fruit — maybe not perfectly, but genuinely.

Let's pray for ourselves and all believers, that we refuse ritualistic, superficial religious acts motivated and empowered by the flesh — fake fruit — and insist on bearing real fruit that proceeds from our living relationship with Jesus. Effective prayer depends on this.

Father,

It is so easy to fall into the trap of fake fruit-bearing. We get so busy we don't find time to be in the Word. The kids get sick, or we have a series of car problems that demand our attention. Then other things come up, and before we know it, the relationship with You gets cooler and more distant. To keep face, we continue doing what other believers expect from us; but the joy is gone, the power is gone, and prayer is affected.

Allowing traditions to influence our lives may sometimes be good, but there is always the danger of relying on what has always been done, or what always has been taught, and allowing those things to take precedence over what Scripture teaches — hoping to substitute these fake fruits for real ones. Father, in our heart of hearts we know that if we do this, we can find ourselves more concerned with what people expect from us than with our relationship with Christ. We can so easily look for approval from people rather than approval from You.

Please forgive us for looking to the fake fruit in our lives to give us assurance that all is well. We want REAL fruit that results from REAL relationship. We long to cling to You like a branch to a vine.

Day 85

———————— *Jesus replied, "I tell you the truth, if you* ————————
have faith and do not doubt, not only
can you do what was done to the fig tree
but also you can say to this mountain, 'Go
throw yourself into the sea,' and it will be
done. If you believe, you will receive
whatever you ask for in prayer."
— Matthew 21:21-22

The **first** conditional prayer promise is in John 16:23-24. Ask in Jesus's name.

The **second** is in John 15:7. Ask while remaining in Him and His Word in you.

The **third** is in John 15:16. Ask as a fruit-bearing believer.

The **fourth** is found here in Matt. 21:21-22. Ask in faith. Remember the confusion I described in the introduction of this book about how anyone could possibly have enough faith to order a mountain thrown into the sea? The fig tree seemed maybe a little less of a problem, but moving mountains was impossible.

In understanding what Christ meant, it helps to understand that Matthew chapters 21-28 deal with the last week before the crucifixion. Among other events of the week, Jesus drives the moneychangers out of the temple (21:12), heals the blind and the lame (21:14), and enters direct confrontation with Israel's leaders (21:15-16). He spends the night in Bethany, and on His way back to Jerusalem, finds a fig tree with no fruit on it, only leaves. He curses the tree and the next morning it is withered. His disciples are amazed and ask how this happened so fast. It's at this point in the narrative that Jesus makes the promise in the text above.

There are two main interpretations of Matt. 21:21-22: The first is to understand these verses as *hyperbole* — that is, great exaggeration to make a point. When we say, "I'm so hungry I could eat a horse," we are using hyperbole. In this view, Jesus is saying if we have faith and don't doubt, we can see God do humanly impossible things through our prayer.

The other view is to see these verses as *symbolic*. Kyle Huntsinger, Youth pastor in Chapin, SC, suggests the fig tree represents Israel's religious system, which was producing no real fruit, but had deteriorated into a form of religion with no real connection to God. And the mountain, probably in view as Christ and the disciples walked toward it, was representative of the temple mount where He had just driven out the moneychangers. As believers pray in faith for the Kingdom to come, they will ultimately see the "fig tree" of a spiritually bankrupt Israel withered; and the "mountain" of a corrupt temple cast down, as Rev. 16:18-20; Amos 9:9; and Is. 2:2 describe.

Prayer is not about doing sensational things for the sake of their own shock and awe. There's no merit in pointlessly ordering literal mountains and fig trees around. The conditional prayer promise of Matt. 21:22 is in the context of doing Christ's work, and faith is absolutely essential to prayer's effectiveness.

There is a caveat, though. As great and as necessary as faith is in prayer, it does not stand alone. The seven conditional prayer promises where God tells us to ask for anything and He will give it *all work in tandem with one another.* We can't choose to claim just one and throw the other six to the wind. The seven great conditional prayer promises form one cohesive whole. They complement and complete each other. They form the boundaries of certain prevailing prayer. Faith is the binding agent that holds them all together in one over-arching truth.

Father,

Thank You for Your insight into one of the more cryptic prayer promises. Help us to understand and meet the condition of this particular promise.

But help us realize all seven of these promises are held in tandem — like a team of horses pulling a carriage — with faith the necessary component in them all.

Day 86

Dear friends, if our hearts do not
ondemn us, we have confidence before
God and receive from him anything we
ask, because we obey his commands
and do what pleases him.
— 1 John 3:21-22

The **first** conditional prayer promise is in John 16:23,24. Ask in Jesus's name.

The **second** is in John 15:7. Ask while remaining in Him.

The **third** is in John 15:16. Ask as a fruit-bearing believer.

The **fourth** is in Matt. 21:22. Ask with faith in Christ and the Word

The **fifth** place where God gives us the conditional promise of receiving anything we ask is "if our hearts do not condemn us" (1 John 3:21-22).

One of the ministries of the Holy Spirit within us is to speak to us in our heart-of-hearts about sin. He urges us to confess these sins, and repent of them; that is, admit what they are, ask for forgiveness, and make a U-turn away from them back to the LORD's leading. This is an every-day experience for all God's children, and the Holy Spirit's role is somewhat like the parental, training role we play in our own children's lives. We know our children still have lots to learn. They are not as mature as we would like them to be. There are some areas that need particular attention. But they are not currently defying our correction — so the relationship between us and them is not strained at the moment. We know they are a work in process.

But the prevailing prayer that this promise refers to is a different scenario. Often, as we approach the Mercy Seat, the Holy Spirit brings **specific sins** to our attention. We sense there is something wrong between us and the LORD, because the Holy Spirit is convicting us of something that grieves the Father greatly. But like willful children, we have insisted on hanging onto that specific sin. When we do this, we place an obstacle between our prayer and the answers God will give if we are willing to repent.

God does not demand sinless perfection when we come to Him in prayer; He knows we are frail as dust, and He pities us (Ps. 103:13-14). *But the bar is higher for the intercessor to whom God hands a blank, signed check, with the promise the intercessor can fill it in as he pleases.* This privilege comes with the responsibility to submit to the Holy Spirit regarding the specific sin He brings to our mind as we are praying.

So, let's keep short accounts. Let's confess our trespasses daily. It's important for many reasons, but it's critically important in prayer, because we "receive from him anything we ask" (1 John 3:22) if we present our prayer with no conviction of sin ignored.

Let's pray for ourselves and all believers that we would mourn anything that comes between us and God during prayer; that we respond in confession and true repentance when the Holy Spirit convicts us of specific sin as we are praying.

Father,

We are certainly aware of how unresolved sin erodes commu-nication in even human relationships — how much more in our communion with You! You show patience to us and forgive a mountain of sin in our lives when we confess it and repent; but You will not grant us the right to ask You for anything, with the promise of giving it to us, when we stubbornly refuse to yield to the Holy Spirit's conviction during a time when we should be the most honest and contrite — when we are in prayer with You! Often, what You convict us of during prayer is surprisingly small.

Day 87

*This is the assurance we have in
pproaching God: that if we ask anything
according to his will, he hears us. And if
we know that he hears us — whatever we ask
— we know that we have what we asked of him.*
— 1 John 5:14-15

The **first** conditional promise is in John 16:23, 24. Ask in Jesus's name.

The **second** is in John 15:7. Ask while remaining in Him and His Word remaining in You.

The **third** is in John 15:16. Ask as a fruit-bearing believer.

The **fourth** is in Matt. 21:22. Ask with faith in Christ and the Word.

The **fifth** is in 1 John 3:21, 22. Ask with no conviction of sin left unresolved.

Today we look at the **sixth** place the New Testament tells us God will give us anything we ask — if we meet the conditions for the promise in 1 John 5:14-15, "ask according to His will."

First John 5:14-15 is aligned with the "Your will be done, on earth as it is in heaven" (Matt. 6:10b) section of the model prayer. It is also aligned with spiritual, eternal issues. When we pray according to the sovereign will of the sovereign God, the answer is always yes or wait. Of course, one of the difficulties in our minds regarding this type of prayer is in discerning whether our requests are according to the will of God or not.

We have two infallible resources to help us make this discernment: The first is the Scriptures. If we can find chapter and verse to back up what we pray for (interpreted in context), we can be sure we are praying according to the will of the God who wrote them. For instance, if we are praying for someone to be cured of cancer — we can pray a prayer of petition, asking for the LORD to heal them; but there are no portions of Scripture saying it is God's will to heal a specific person of a specific disease — so we must pray, as Jesus did in Luke 22:42 KJV, "nevertheless not my will, but thine, be done." On the other hand, we can pray for healing (a petition) but also pray specific Scripture for them: That this person be comforted (2 Cor. 1:3-5), that they would cast their cares on the LORD (1 Pet. 5:7), that God would work everything together for their good (Rom. 8:18) and many others. When we are praying these specific Scriptures, we are without doubt praying squared up with God's will and can know we have what we ask.

Second, believers have the resource of the indwelling Holy Spirit Who brings specific people and issues to mind that need prayer. Then He intercedes "for us with groans that words cannot express" (Romans 8:26-27). He works on our prayer and makes it acceptable. He motivates, enables, and leads us in how we should pray when we are unsure.

This is a fantastic quote about the Holy Spirit's work in us as we pray:

"The eternal decrees of God project their shadows over the hearts of godly men [mankind] in the form of prayer. What God intends to do he tells unto his servants by inclining them to ask him to do what he himself is resolved to do. God says, 'do this and that'; but then adds, 'For this I will be enquired of by the house of Israel." (Ez. 36:37)

— C.H. Spurgeon

Please pray for the Church generally and us specifically, that we have God-given discernment about prayer; that we recognize and depend on the Holy Spirit's enablement and the Scripture's guidance as we endeavor to pray according to God's will.

Father,

Your Word does not lessen what we can pray for — it enormously, even infinitely, expands it — because Your Holy Spirit and Your eternal decrees and purposes for ultimate good are brought to bear on the subject. Help us to pray for all people and all needs; for all situations and trials; for all things — aligned with Your Word, because it expresses Your will. And in doing this, we bring the desperate needs of people and commit them to Your infinite, eternal sufficiency. O Father. Help us to grasp the wonder of this opportunity in prayer.

Day 88

And I will do whatever you
ask in my name, so that the Son
may bring glory to the Father.
You may ask me for anything
in my name, and I will do it.
— John 14:13-14

The **first** conditional promise is in John 16:23, 24. Ask in Jesus's name.

The **second** is in John 15:7. Ask while remaining in Him with His Word remaining in you.

The **third** is in John 15:16. Ask as a fruit-bearing believer.

The **fourth** is in Matt. 21:22. Ask with faith in Christ and the Word.

The **fifth** is in 1 John 3:21, 22. Ask with no conviction of sin left unresolved.

The **sixth** is in 1 John 5:14, 15. Ask according to the will of God.

The **seventh** conditional prayer promise is in John 14:13-14 where it indicates asking in Jesus's name is connected to His purpose of bringing glory to the Father. If we want God to give us whatever we ask in prayer, we must pray with the same purpose — to see the Father glorified. Praying in the name of Jesus is linked in these verses to praying with the same motivation that Jesus has. Whatever we pray for, whoever we pray for, we must ask for it *because we want the whole world to recognize the immense, awesome, splendid, brilliant, majestic HEAVY WEIGHT OF WORTH that is God's alone. We want His glory to be displayed in answering our prayer.*

Motives are extremely important to God. But keeping our motives pure in prayer is like wearing white clothes in a barnyard — they get dirtied easily. We tend to let our own desires take preeminence when we pray. Sometimes, like spoiled children, we want what we want, with no thought of God's perfect plans.

There is a time and place for expressing our desires to God; His fatherly heart invites us to do that in our petitions. But we must honestly be able to say, "Father, if this petition I'm asking doesn't cause others to recognize Your worth — Your glory — then I'd rather not have it. Your glory is what is eternally important — not my personal desires."

Just as little children accept the decision that they are not old enough at the age of ten for a motorbike and submit their desire for one to the wisdom, love, and resources of their earthly father — we must submit our desires to what brings God glory in this present age, for that is what will bring the very best for us in the end. It is God's power, sovereignty, omnipotence, and omniscience, etc. — the attributes of His being that make up His enormous weight of worth (His glory) — that make it possible for Him to give us the eternally valuable desires of our heart. Mature faith is willing to trust and wait.

Let's pray that we keep a tight rein on our motives when we pray — that we truly desire for God to be recognized for His infinite WORTH in every petition we raise to Him.

Father,

Let us comprehend what the conditional prayer promise of John 14:13-14 is about. May the attitude of our hearts in prayer be the same as Hab. 2:14 KJV — that we desire for the whole earth to be "filled with the knowledge of the glory of the LORD as the waters cover the sea." Father, help us to see that Your glory is what will make Heaven really Heaven.

Day 89

Hear my voice when I call, O Lord; be
merciful to me and answer me. My heart says
of you, "Seek his face!" Your face, Lord I will seek.
— Psalm 27:7-8

The **first** conditional promise is in John 16:23-24. Ask in Jesus's name.

The **second** is in John 15:7. Ask while remaining in Him and His Word in you.

The **third** is in John 15:16. Ask as a fruit-bearing believer.

The **fourth** is in Matt. 21:22. Ask with faith in Christ and the Word.

The **fifth** is in 1 John 3:21-22. Ask with no conviction of sin left unresolved.

The **sixth** is in 1 John 5:14-15. Ask according to the will of God.

The **seventh** is in John 14:13-14. Ask motivated by desire for God's glory.

I am sitting in front of a computer as I write this entry. The machine is turned on. The screen looks right: Everything is working as it should at the moment. I know I have pulled up the right file; I know I am pushing the right keys on the keyboard for the entry to be recorded; I know I am connected to the internet; I know the computer is getting electricity and I know the electric line to the house is operational. If the screen suddenly goes blank, I know there is a problem, and I start investigating which of the components and connections necessary to the operation of the computer are disconnected or defunct.

Like the different components that need to be in operation for a computer to work, the seven conditional prayer promises are components of asking God for *anything* and having His promise of receiving it. The promises are boundaries, or parameters, within which His promise is extended. If we are not sensing prayer being answered, we should start investigating which of these boundaries is being transgressed. We need to address the problem and fix it.

The conditional prayer promises were never meant to be treated like diamonds locked in a safe — valued, but never used. We could read them and struggle with the concepts — and don't misunderstand — that is a good thing to do; but they must be more than that. We could even memorize these promises, treasuring them in our souls — and that is an even better thing to do — yet that's still not enough! Unless these great conditional prayer promises are set ablaze with yielding to the Holy Spirit's work in us, they remain tantalizing, but out of reach. Unless the Spirit is submitting our prayer to God, there is a vital missing component in the process.

We should certainly pray within the parameters of the conditional prayer promises — but may we learn this: They are promises to plead, rather than techniques to be mastered or demands to be met. Prayer is a living, breathing, warm, intimate interchange between us, the Holy Spirit, Jesus our Advocate, and God the Father. All of us, the Father, the Son, the Holy Spirit and the believer are in tune with the intercessions.

The Spirit is a Spirit of life as well as truth, and the first thing that he always does is to make everything living and vital. And, of course, there is all the difference in the world between the life and the liveliness produced by the Spirit and the kind of artifact, the bright and breezy imitation, produced by people.

— *Living Water*
Martyn Lloyd-Jones

O, Church:
When we sense the Holy Spirit calling us to seek
God in prayer, may we, like the Psalmist, say,
"Your face, Lord, will I seek." (Ps. 27:8)

Day 90

And pray in the Spirit on all occasions
with all kinds of prayers and requests. With
this in mind, be alert and always keep
on praying for all the saints.
— *Ephesians 6:18*

Music functions under set, crucial principles that govern its practice and progress. These principles must be in place for the four-year-old child who is just learning at the family piano as well as for the accomplished virtuoso at Carnegie Hall.

Prayer, too, has over-arching principles that govern its practice and effectiveness. Although Scripture says an enormous amount about prayer, we could condense these principles into seven critical precepts that help us understand the structure and practice of New Testament prayer.

The first governing principle is the model prayer in Matt. 6:5-15. In it we learn the topics for prayer: communing with God in praise, worship, and thanksgiving; interceding for His Kingdom and His will; asking for our personal needs; confessing sin, asking forgiveness, and requesting protection from evil.

The second governing principle is the relationship all prayer is built upon — its bedrock. We do not pray alone — nor on our own merit. We are heard in prayer because of *relationship*. That is, the Holy Spirit initiates salvation, indwells the believer, and motivates prayer; the believer is in Christ; Christ is in God; Christ is seated at the right hand of God the Father where He makes continual intercession for us; and *we are seated with Him and invited to offer up prayer in unity with Him.* This relationship of unity with the Triune God, this incredible spiritual reality, is the bedrock of prayer. All effective New Testament prayer is built on it.

The third governing principle, absolutely critical to prayer that can ask God for anything, are the conditional prayer promises. Like marriage, we are admonished not to enter into prayer unadvisedly. Prayer is serious business that demands commitment. Prayer may start as only the cry of a new-born believer, but it grows and develops and turns into weighty, eternal interactions. God does not commit His power to careless, slothful petitioners. He does, however, give that omnipotent power to those who endeavor to pray in Jesus's name, abide in Him, bear fruit, ask in faith, confess sin, and repent when convicted during prayer; then align their prayer with His revealed will, and desire God's glory. When we are within the boundaries of these promises in our petitions, it is safe for God to trust us with His omnipotence.

In the fourth governing principle, is a Biblical pattern to answered prayer. Search the Scriptures and we will see where God promises something — He burdens someone to pray for the promise — and He answers above and beyond anything the petitioner originally intended. We learn a great prayer lesson in this fourth principle — O, that we would search the Bible for His promises to us and then pray for them.

The fifth governing principle is the attitude of the supplicant. Humility and honesty are absolute necessities — their lack is a deal-breaker. We can talk to God about anything, we can pour out our hearts to him (Ps. 62:8) but we'd best be humble and honest.

The purpose of prayer is the sixth governing principle. There are many facets to God's purpose in prayer, but a major one is that God is bringing us into the circle of unity, fellowship, and common purposes with Himself — which is surely the golden vial all other purposes are preserved in.

The last governing principle is a simple one: *We must pray.* Like the child who sits at the piano and plays according to overarching principles he is learning, but not yet fully aware of, we must pray whether we understand it all or not. And the Holy Spirit, divine and loving teacher that He is, will motivate, enable, and lead us to pray. Great will be the reward in Heaven.

Father,

We would love to have it all together — to understand all that You teach on prayer and practice it faithfully. Would You help us in this regard? Will You give us a great army of contemporary saints who won't give You any rest until You establish "Jerusalem and [make] her the praise of the earth" (Is. 62:7) which is one of Your ultimate goals in Revelation 21 and 22?

We ask that You do what You must do in us to call Your Church to Your Throne of Grace in continual prayer.

We ask that You comfort and make Your presence very real, even in miraculous ways, to the persecuted believers who refuse to deny Your name.

We ask that You give us "grace to help in time of need" (Heb. 4:16 KJV).

We ask that You purify and sanctify Your people.

We ask that lies be exposed, and truth revealed.

We ask that Your people patiently persevere, regardless of what happens in these last days before Jesus comes again.

We ask that You open blind eyes, unstop deaf ears, and enlighten minds to turn to Christ as savior and put their hope in Him.

We ask in unified voice with Rev. 22:20, "Even so, come Lord Jesus."

We ask that You show us how to pray.

And we ask these things in the name of Jesus. Amen.

Summary

And God raised us up with Christ
and seated us with him in the
heavenly realms in Christ Jesus, in
order that in the coming ages he might
show the incomparable riches of his
grace, expressed in his kindness
to us in Christ Jesus.
— Ephesians 2:6-7

True prayer never evaporates. It is so valued by God that He preserves it (Rev. 5:8). True prayer is always answered — sometimes "yes," sometimes "no," and sometimes "wait." But it is always answered. And true prayer is the intimate, working, communicating, loving partnership between the Triune God and His army of saints who still reside on this present earth — it is their direct line to Command Headquarters.

Just think of it. Almighty God has ordained, according to Eph. 2:6-7, that believers have the insurmountable privilege to sit with Christ in His seat at the right hand of the God of the Universe and comingle our prayer with His. We are invited (and commanded!) to be actively involved in praying down the "immeasurable riches of his grace in kindness toward us in Christ Jesus" (Eph. 2:7).

Every believer sits uniquely placed — by the sovereign plan of God

— in a positional, spiritual reality where we have responsibility to pray for those in our own sphere of Kingdom work. It's a job that's been assigned only to us. No one can pray in our particular sphere but us.

It's up to us to pray for the needs of the Church. Using military lingo, it's our job to see that the Church is not without power, not without supply, not without communication, not without weapons, not without direction, not without soldiers, not without protection, and not without focus for the spiritual warfare that rages all around us. It's up to us to pray for hurting, suffering people and ask for the application of the promises the LORD has given His children to assist them during their days in this present world.

Today's hurting churches groan in anguish for the saints to get a vision of what God intends prayer to accomplish. Believers need the whole vision as revealed in the whole spectrum of Scripture — from Genesis to Revelation.

Stale, rote, traditional prayer is of little value. The church desperately needs more — it needs the power of the Triune God which is obtained at the Throne of Grace as we pray for the promises and according to the Word. Apathetic prayer won't get the job done. Neither will self-focused prayer. The Church needs saints — in John Piper's words — with a "wartime mentality," because we are engaged in great spiritual conflict that affects all people for all eternity.

We are living in a time where people all across the globe are frightened. Our Young people are confused and anxious. Our churches are struggling against the spirit of antichrist. But here is a spectacular and comforting truth: God has an unlimited source of wisdom, power, and provision for us. We avail ourselves of it only when we pray. He is calling His saints to the task.

C.A. Archer

God has seated us with Jesus in the
Heavenlies. It is our joy, privilege,
delight and duty to join Him in continual intercession
with the Father — asking that God's infinitely good, and
perfect, and life-giving will be done in all things.

267

New Testament Text-to-Day Cross References

<u>Matthew</u>

5:44-45	Day 79
6:6	Day 21
6:7	Day 13
6:9a	Day 2; Day 3
6:9b	Day 4
6:10	Day 5
6:11	Day 6
6:12	Day 7
6:13	Day 8
7:7-8	Day 23
9:37-38	Day 73
21:13	Day 42
21:21-22	Day 85
25:21	Day 45

Hebrews

4:16	Day 25; Day 70
7:25	Day 52
13:3	Day 28; Day 41

James

4:2b	Day 71
4:3	Day 15
5:14-15	Day 72
5:16	Day 62

1 Peter

1:7	Day 53
2:9	Day 34
4:7	Day 38

1 John

| 3:21-22 | Day 9; Day 86 |
| 5:14-15 | Day 87 |

Jude

| 1:20 | Day 30 |

Old Testament Text-to-Day Cross References